A time to live, a time to die. By Jacqui Ryalls.
1st edition published November 1999.
2nd edition published 2012.

If you would like Jacqui to come and share her powerful testimony
Please contact her direct on jryalls@toucansurf.com

Matador
9 Priory Business Park,
Wistow Road, Kibworth Beauchamp,
Leicestershire. LE8 0RX
Tel: (+44) 116 279 2299
Fax: (+44) 116 279 2277
Email: books@troubador.co.uk
Web: www.troubador.co.uk/matador

ISBN 978 1780881 515

British Library Cataloguing in Publication Data.
A catalogue record for this book is available from the British Library.

Typeset in 12pt Adobe Garamond Pro by Troubador Publishing Ltd, Leicester, UK

Matador is an imprint of Troubador Publishing Ltd
Printed in the UK by TJ International, Padstow, Cornwall

A Time
TO LIVE
A Time
TO DIE

A Time
TO LIVE
A Time
TO DIE

JACQUI RYALLS

To everything there is a season,
A time for every purpose under heaven:
A time to live and a time to die;
A time to plant, and a time to pluck what is planted;
A time to weep, and a time to laugh;
A time to mourn, and a time to dance;
A time to love, and a time to hate;
A time of war, and a time of peace.

Ecclesiastes 3 1-8

Dedication

This book has been dedicated with deep appreciation to my husband Paul, who has given me the gift of friendship, much more than I deserved.

I thank him for the freedom he has given me by allowing me to grow within the safe space of his love. May his eyes continue to be veiled from my weeds, and may he continue to look for the flowers within our relationship.

I trust that through reading this book, he and the reader will realise that Paul is my hero. He has totally underpinned the work with his constant support, love and friendship. He has my love and respect much more than he can know.

This work is also offered with much love and deep appreciation to all our family, friends and supporters especially to our youngest son Richard, who during the war years willingly opened his heart in unselfish love, by allowing us the space to love an ever-growing Bosnian family.

To each person who has touched our lives:
Please receive this offering as a gift, in the clearest truth I can express from within myself.

Please find yourselves within the pages. We have tried to honour your loving support, by being your hands and your feet in support of the war victims of Bosnia.

Contents

Introduction

These words were penned in 1980.

"To be moved to put pen to paper is like not being able to find the paper quickly enough before the thoughts go! Often, I have been willing to share the deep part of myself only to recoil from fear of being ridiculed."

For each one of us the very spark of life, the inspiration is in the now. We can be people of the now. What we are, what we have to give away of ourselves is the gift.

We can miss the opportunity or block the moment, unwilling to relate openly to those around us for fear of being judged.

Over the years many have asked, 'When are you going to write the book?'

Each time I responded. "Probably only when I am old and grey and in a wheelchair."

Each of us has a story, each is unique, yet the movement around us can infiltrate our space and the pure inner move within our spirit can simply get lost.

It wasn't that I ever wanted to write a book, it was that I was unable to give full witness of the awesome, almighty God that I have come to know and trust, without writing it.

What I also discovered in 1993 when I started to write was that the 'I' kept getting in the way. I became ashamed of my imperfections and desired more of the 'living waters.'

The more we heard people say, 'Aren't you brave,' the more Paul and I questioned our motives. Our simple desire was to follow the Holy Spirit's leading and try to help a people who were trying to survive in the extreme circumstance of war.

In some ways this book is about survival, about constant choice. A choice that is open to each one of us who are prepared to roll up our sleeves to battle against hypocrisy, selfish motive and the constant desire for self-gratification, power or glory... all of which... I have been guilty.

So maybe only those who are willing to check and re-check their own motives will begin to penetrate any understanding of this call and work and therefore be available to carry it forward into the future.

So for me the need to continue to fight that negative spirit which can so easily take hold in our lives is still of the utmost priority. Are we willing to forgive? Are we willing to grow? Are we willing to become a more finely honed tool in the hand of God?

I pray all who read this book will do so with an open mind and be encouraged to 'go for it.' Roll up your sleeves and become 'love in action' and experience the faithful God who wants us all to fulfil His purpose for our lives on this earth before it's too late.

JR.

CHAPTER 1

The Wake Up Call

"… and he is looking for one hundred vehicles to take aid to refugees in Croatia," came the words droning over the radio as I listened with only half an antennae directed towards the worldly sound waves.

Trying to ignore the whole report I looked across at Paul, my husband, who by this time was blissfully enjoying his rest, cocooned in the warm, sweet smelling sheets, with his head resting on the edge of the cream satin pillows. He, like most men in time honoured-fashion, was asleep with a look of complete contentment on his kindly, bearded face.

"…and I heard the audible voice of God," continued the interviewee on the airwaves in autumn 1992.

Snuggling into the warmth, and trying to settle down by bending my body around the contours of my relatively new husband, I tried not to listen, but was unknowingly hooked by the inciting message and dulcet tones.

The interviewer continued; "And you are looking to raise a convoy of one hundred vehicles to travel across Europe and meet on the outskirts of Slovenia?"

"Yes, that's right," he continued, "anyone who could bring any kind of vehicle full of food and clothes for the refugees in the camps out there, contact me. These people have lost their homes and have nothing. The trip should take about two weeks. If there is anybody out there listening, who thinks they could help…"

"Wake up Paul," I urgently insisted, giving him a sharp dig in the ribs for good measure.

"What, what's the matter?" he struggled to focus his mind on returning to planet earth.

"This is just right for you. You've always wanted to go to the Congo or something. Your van is sitting outside and you've always wanted to do something worthwhile. Well, this will suit you down to the ground!"

Having already grasped the vision of hundreds of lorries, vans, trailers, and in fact all sorts of vehicles rolling across Europe, I tried again. I was confident that Paul's response would be one of placating me, in the hope of being allowed the opportunity of returning back to the land of nod, at least without any more irrational ideas being hurled at him at this late hour.

"Imagine, one huge convoy of hope weaving its way through all those countries," I continued, actually seeing the scene in my mind's eye.

"What are you talking about Jacqui? Go to sleep and stop being a pain!" Paul bit back. By now he was beginning to show signs of really not appreciating being 'got at' at this unearthly hour.

"No, seriously, this is just right for you. Listen!" Much to Paul's irritation, I jumped out of bed and scrambled to find a pen and paper to write down the contact number. He turned his back, grabbing the bedclothes as a form of defence and protest.

"Seriously," I insisted, "this really is just for you. We will send off in the morning for the details, I've got the number." I knew I was now pushing the boundaries and was quite triumphant at pulling such an opportunity off the conveyor belt of life as it passed my vision, especially as I wasn't even looking. Little did we realise at the time, that everything we had been through in life had been the preparation, which had led us to this very moment.

The first chess piece was now in position, our lives were about to take on a new almighty dimension. Almighty being His operative word, after all, isn't this what Christians expect when they pray, 'Lord here I am, available for you?'

Next morning, in a more conscious state, Paul had no trouble agreeing that it all sounded very feasible, possible, and even quite exciting. I assured him, although I was only just out of hospital after major surgery, that I would do everything possible to get behind him and help him join the convoy, if that was what he felt he would like to do.

It only needed a few phone calls for us to fill Paul's van with aid. We didn't need to reach out very far as most of the help came from our immediate neighbours, family and friends who were happy to support such a venture.

Our biggest problem was transport, for although our home had all the hallmarks of more affluent times; we now lived very modestly, supported by Paul's plumbing work.

We had both been married before and Paul understood my need for inner healing from the emotional scars which inevitably we bring into new relationships. I was however, by this time, learning to trust him. For Paul was a straight forward answer to my prayer. It's also fair to say, it was Paul's unquestioning love over the years, which gradually allowed the child within me to receive some healing.

Although my early memories of childhood were fragmented, I could still recall as a four year old a few scenes from the period 1943-1945, when many of us children were evacuated from industrial cities. I had been placed with a variety of different families during the war years, as our Mother needed to work to support the family, which indirectly freed my Father to play away from home. Nevertheless, it was my Father who had fetched me back from one family, when he discovered I had been sleeping six in a bed with other children, and that my new shoes had been given to the daughter of the household.

On returning home I could remember my sense of shame because the hem of my dress was showing four inches below my coat, such an indiscretion in the eyes of our Mother.

In contrast, for another period I lived with a bank manager and his wife in the south of England and could still visualise the bright colours and intricate patterns in the beautifully embroidered tablecloths stacked in piles on the dining room table. I could recall licking the ends of my fingers, so as to taste the sweet nectar from the jar of honey strategically placed at my height by the french windows.

Apparently that couple had wanted to adopt me but on hearing of the proposed plans, again I was hastily brought home, but this time by my Mother. I had often wondered who the couple were and if they were still alive?

After this near change of fate, I was promptly dispatched to live with an aunt who was eventually to become the Matron of Broadmoor, which at the time was Britain's top security hospital. In later years I would have trained to become a nurse, had my formidable aunt not insisted that I should follow in her footsteps. This would have meant nursing highly disturbed patients. So, in spite of the desires of others, my path was held within the family unit to run its God-given course in time.

By the end of 1945 our parents declared a 'new start' and I could remember as a five-year-old being awe-struck by the spectacular colours of the autumn trees as my elder brother and I were driven by taxi through the beautiful Wye Valley. We went to live in the Anchor Hotel, Tintern, where our mother took the job as head cook which earned our accommodation whilst Father worked away in Chepstow. I was not quite sure if it was our parents' intention that Father stayed away, but even at that age I thought... he seldom comes home.

For my brother and I, we at least had two years in the glorious Wye Valley, where our lives were idyllic. I could still recall the sweet-smelling hay and the soft, pale coloured primroses as I spent hours soaking up the beautiful presence of something awesome and very special, in the atmosphere of the Abbey nearby.

But back in the city of my birth, Coventry, in 1947 it was hard to find any beauty in our surroundings. We all lived above a cobbler's shop where our Father kept greyhounds for racing. The kennels were only accessible down an open iron fire escape, which stretched from outside our back door down to ground level. The dread of my life was for my Father to ask me to feed the hounds when he was late for work, which was most days. I became quite skilled at jumping down the last five steps without spilling too much of the sloppy, foul smelling concoction of food. The fear and sense of dread I experienced has been indelibly inscribed in my mind. I would hurl my body forward, and run the gauntlet through packs of giant rats that seemed to wait daily to taunt my childhood frame.

The grey upstairs bathroom doubled as a kitchen and my brother and I needed to sit on the edge of the bath to eat at the old kitchen table. Any attempt to touch the saucepan of boiling water on the stove nearby without a cloth in hand, would frequently produce a severe electric shock.

My lot was to sleep in a single, black iron bed in the same room as our parents and because I found the black bars on my bed so ugly I used to decorate them with bows, which I made from the silver paper found in cigarette packets. The little bed, however, did afford me the protection to hide under the bedclothes when my Father returned home in the early hours. It didn't seem to take him long to find reasons to fly into a rage and tip up the double bed if my Mother dared to refuse to turn over... for what, I had no idea in that age of innocence.

In the daytime there were times when I would hide behind the green settee clutching my pet greyhound for protection. From this vantage point one Sunday afternoon, I could see our Father standing there the worse for drink, raging, with thick red blood running from the corner of his mouth. Mother, although able to hold her own verbally, for once retaliated physically, and to everyone's shock threw a pot of boiling tea straight towards Father. I must have blanked the rest, but looking back it was hardly surprising that as a chronic asthmatic, I missed half my schooling. I left school seemingly only knowing that the battle of Hastings was 1066. Nevertheless, I inherited much from Mother's strength of character and thankfully I have never lost that sense of who I am on the inside, which was to become my most precious inheritance.

Yet my emotional development had barely got started, when at the age of twenty-five I glanced across a crowded dance floor, where the sound of the band playing, 'Strangers in the night' did little to make me aware that the life and death pain of every emotion was just a dance away. With this one glance a chemical reaction had been ignited and in a moment of time, without either of us realising it, the man standing in front of me was to become the very purpose of my life for the next twenty years.

Soon I would worship the very ground on which he walked. I had to learn the hard way that although he did not realise it, he held the ultimate balance of power in the relationship, which for the survival of the subsequent marriage, proved to be emotionally disastrous for us both.

Over the years I had plenty of opportunity to get well acquainted with the negative oppressive spirit which was never far away. There is a state of helplessness; a place of darkness relating to emotional bondage and our added emotional addiction and co-dependency on each other, was as lethal as any addiction to drugs or alcohol.

Neither of us could understand why the ups were sheer ecstasy and the downs were so dark. We both teetered on continuous emotional pain and both failed to get in touch with what was taking place within the relationship.

Again, following Mother's pattern, I began to feel used. Over the years the more I worked in business and successfully provided the trappings of a more comfortable lifestyle, the more my success highlighted the imbalance in the relationship. The lack of appreciation meant that the resentment grew and so did my outbursts of anger in frequency and verbosity. The more we tried to move ourselves out of the painful situation, the more we were both consumed by guilt and, sadly, I was sure that some of the unresolved guilt feelings from the conflicts were passed on to our children.

During a particularly difficult time within the marriage I met a young lady whilst walking in a park, who told me that two thousand years earlier Jesus Christ, the Son of God had been crucified on the cross for my sins. It turned out that the babe I had been told about at school, who was born in a manger, and who was crucified on the green hill, had something to do with me directly.

Apparently, if I was willing to accept in my heart that there actually was a Father in heaven who did care enough about me, then on repentance of sins I could be forgiven. The whole experience of surrendering my heart to an unseen God, felt much like being asked to jump off the edge of a cliff with only an umbrella to save me, but, after much wrestling within, I made the absolute choice by faith. I accepted that God was real. That Jesus Christ was in fact the Son of God and He had hung on the cross for my sins. I knew that most of all I wanted to develop a relationship with Him and discover what He wanted with my life.

It was therefore no surprise that in the end, my husband asked me to make another choice which would change my life and, consequently, thousands of others.

"Jacqui, choose between me and your relationship with Jesus."

"Please don't ask me to make that choice," I implored, knowing the final battle lines had been drawn.

So, after sixteen years of marriage, the 'Stranger in the night' left the matrimonial home, which in turn placed each of us on opposite sides of the spiritual divide.

When we had moved into our last country home together, there were three children, four horses, two dogs, two goats and several cats, even a swimming pool; yet, within an eighteen-month period, I found myself completely, physically alone. "Lord you only have to let Satan send the boils," I challenged out of a place of despair. So why was I surprised a few weeks later when the doctors told me that the lump in my breast which was the size of a golf ball was cancerous?

Thankfully the lump was soon dealt with through surgery but for nearly four years I crawled through the valley of the shadow of death, mourning everything I had said or done as I unknowingly continued through the refining process. I teetered on the edge of destruction, being tempted by thoughts to end it all, verses my gut determination for survival. I hung onto life by my fingernails and with faith only the size of a mustard seed, I struggled to come out of the emotional addiction for my then, ex-husband. Finally having surrendered another layer in my heart, and giving away all the shares in my profitable business along with most of our worldly goods, I determined to trust God completely.

By 1984, age forty-four I sat in bed-sit-land, staring at my total wealth of four, ten pound notes and thought, "Well girl, for a half intelligent person, you are totally mental. Eighteen months ago you were driving a Porsche...now you don't even have a home for your son." I braced myself, pulled myself up and cried out in some anguish.

"OK, Lord... I give in... You lead and I'll follow, but Lord, I really don't want to be alone, so please Lord, could I have a husband who loves you this time... and, Lord if you could manage it... could he please be six foot tall...and a divorcee so that I don't have to follow in the wake of another woman's good footprints?" Several months later I met Paul, and he says that I produced a tape measure to check his height, to make sure he was God's man for me. Thankfully as a God-given gift, Paul has the most buoyant cheerful disposition, a kind friendly nature and is seven years younger than me.

When we were first married, I think it is fair to say that one wouldn't put us together as the perfect match. From the start we both knew that for us to survive as a couple, and create the opportunity for our marriage to mature into a healthy relationship, there would need to be much compromise and learning in every area of matrimonial conflict, especially as we were both running our own businesses with all the daily commitments and subsequent strains that ultimate responsibility produces.

As the years began to pass and whilst a deep love and affection had begun to grow between us, in my last two years in business I knew inside myself that I would not be able to carry on punishing my body much longer. At that time I owned two city centre high profile Bridal shops, which also supported two other franchise units. There were days when, as I tried to carry heavy bridal gowns, my legs would seize up and I would only be able to move like a beached whale.

It became clear that I would have no option but to accept and let go of a way of life that was taking its toll on us both physically, emotionally and certainly spiritually. So the ever growing pain proved to be a sign post that gave me the impetus to close the business in the least damaging way to all concerned. It took several difficult months to orchestrate all the necessary moves in financial terms. The decision cost us both personally in every way, but we both gained an inner peace as the complete change in lifestyle was made. I finally became officially retired.

I now had time to explore what was going on inside my body, and after a visit to a top London specialist, thanks to the grace of a friend of mine, I discovered a fall from a horse twenty years earlier had healed, leaving nerves trapped. The discs above and below the area were having to do extra work as the spine had solidified to protect the injured areas.

Today we can now look back over many chapters and know that 'The Potter' had decided it was time to mould our rough old clay together into some sort of useful vessel for His purpose. God had my full attention, but for what?

It was a bright, sunny, winter's day, late in 1992, when Paul and I were enjoying each other's company, giggling and chatting all the way to take Paul's small van to be serviced, in anticipation of his forthcoming trip to the continent. We asked the garage owner to do a good job, as the van was to go out to Croatia. However, we were a little surprised when, having serviced our only means of transport, he held his sides with his large, black, greasy hands and just fell about laughing.

"This van won't get you to the end of the motorway lady, let alone Croatia!" The garage owner exclaimed with what seemed to be some delight.

A little dejected, but now determined, I thought, '*Oh well, we'll see about that!*' By insulting Paul's little van, he was insulting my husband and that in turn was touching my 'Mother Hen' button.

After thirty-five years in business I was used to getting things done and now I needed to tune in at a different level, so added, as if as an after thought, '*If this trip is really in God's plan for Paul, I expect He will provide a vehicle for him to use.*'

At this time I was still nursing the internal and external scars from some major surgery, so going on a trip to Croatia, in convoy, was not in my plans either for convalescence or retirement. But this did not stop me from getting quite frustrated with my own inability to function efficiently with all cylinders blazing. I realised I was still in the 'no lifting, no driving' stage of a six month recuperation period but, I did think that I could make a few phone calls and get things moving a little better than I had so far. However, this time regardless of the frustration, I verbally whipped myself in preference to whipping Paul.

Thankfully, within days, a neighbour had come to the rescue with the offer of a new Transit van, which was a company demonstration model; the only problem was, it had a £2,000 excess on the insurance. Whilst we appreciated the offer, we had no idea how we would ever pay the money if there was to be an accident en route and this, of course, increased the tension between Paul and I. Nevertheless we were grateful for the vehicle and accepted it with much appreciation.

A local paper printed the story of the convoy with Paul's need for a co-driver and we had quite a few phone calls, but began to realise that most of the callers were probably not suitable, as it seemed many just wanted to escape from their own circumstances.

I was very uncomfortable with my discernment in this matter and actually warned Paul, "When the next enquiry comes, ask them what contribution they are prepared to make, apart from their offer of time. Hard work and the need to produce funding have a way of sorting out the men from the boys."

A few days later we received a call from a young man in Bristol who said he wanted to help and had already been in contact with the main group of the 'Convoy of Hope.' The organisers had put him on to Paul, yet immediately we both sensed there was something not quite right about him. Maybe it was nothing, but because of my unease we decided to be a little careful if this man came on the phone again. We had yet to learn, especially in this type of expedition, that any weakness of character would soon show up and cause havoc in a team.

In the meantime a middle-aged accountant, pleasant in manner, came offering his services. We instinctively liked Joe, welcomed him as a co-driver, and excitedly made our initial plans.

Within a few days, and much to my disappointment, the first young man, Freddie, phoned again having collected £160 and still wanting to join the team, but this time he was even more earnest. Paul agreed that we had a problem, but as he was still trying to be fair we decided that the only thing we could do was to try to take two vehicles, which meant we would need to find another driver. Not wishing to fall into 'a weak little woman act' and, as the days were getting short, I agreed to try and drive the 1,000 miles, but I was still surprised to find a great peace flooding my heart.

This decision sent me again into petitioning prayer. "Lord, I'm sorry to come again over this matter of transport and you must know what you were doing sending this young man Freddie to us for a second time." I went on and on, filtering the matter over in my mind until; eventually my heart became quietened and silenced as I responded to the soft, still inner voice.

Through the process I had this deep desire to phone the minister in Coventry who had married us both, and with whom we had a deep spiritual bond. I discovered that his 'first in command', was now working with a group in Leeds, an organisation which was deeply committed to helping Bosnian refugees in this country. With their encouragement and with more confidence now, I contacted the local churches and, within a few days, we had enough funds to hire a second van and enough aid to fill them both.

At no time in retirement had I really envisaged such an adventure. I had plans for long hours in our new little garden catching up on a lifetime of reading the likes of C.T. Studd and Catherine Marshall, to quote extremes. Yet, all of a sudden, having agreed I would go and, much to my own alarm, all the old enthusiasm and energy just burst forth, so I argued. "Lord I don't want to get involved with that world out there any more. I have done my bit; I'm tired and need a rest!" I pounded at the gates of heaven, yet somehow every time I did so, some dear soul arrived at our door with two bags of sugar for Bosnia. Somehow my words just seemed to come back and hit me full in the face…who was I kidding about retirement anyway? Maybe I was just born for the cut and thrust of life and maybe this was the beginning of being obedient to God's will for my life?

*****

By early November 1992, with all the logistics settled, and due to catch the 3am ferry, we agreed a meeting point with the other 240 drivers at a motorway service station in England. Our two transit vans would help make up a full 'Convoy of Hope', all moving across Europe independently, and meeting again in Austria three days later.

I was still tender inside from the surgery but nevertheless, with the excitement of the last minute loading, had decided to put my body on hold for care later. After all what difference would it make? I simply decided none of this pain would inhibit our quest to experience in full, what life had to offer us as a couple under God's authority.

I had to admit that I was vaguely curious to know what pattern God was planning to weave into His tapestry for our lives. What we didn't know yet, was that the main problem of this trip had still to appear. The difficulties started when we naively picked up my co-driver, Freddie. He had hitched a lift to an agreed meeting point. At first we chatted enthusiastically over a cup of tea at a service station.

It didn't take long for us to realise that Freddie was interested in Eastern Religion and we anticipated there might be some clashes of doctrine as our spiritual experiences were entirely different. I didn't have a reputation for suffering fools gladly and, as far as I was concerned, Freddie had little spiritual discernment, so I was indeed beginning to pray for a lot more grace.

When we made our second stop a few hours later, my fears were realised. Freddie and Joe, Paul's co-driver, were soon at each other's throats. Paul, in true conciliatory style, tried to put the bickering down to the late hour.

"Come on you guys, let's learn to work together. We have a long journey ahead."

"Let's draw a line, clear the decks of all that stuff, and start again," I interjected in support.

To enable Freddie and Joe to get to know each other a little better, I suggested that they travel again together over the next stretch of the journey. It seemed a good idea at the time, until we arrived at Dover.

"That's it, that's it!" Joe was now pacing relentlessly up and down the quayside in the dark. He was refusing to go another mile with Freddie. "He's just a nut case, a bloody nut case!" he snorted.

Freddie, by this time, was standing menacingly at the open window on my side of the cab, his finger wagging in my face. His breaths swirled about in the cold night air like that of a fiery dragon. Paul knew from experience Freddie was making a big, big mistake.

"Do something – do something, you bitch!" Freddie snarled, right into my face again. "He says I can't drive. It's all your fault!"

"Really?" I responded very softly, whilst at the same time, slowly and deliberately lifting myself off the seat. I rose about four inches taller and fixed him firmly, eyeball to eyeball. "Why don't you back off friend, back off, now?"

Quickly, Paul tried some light banter again to diffuse the situation but we both knew we had a big problem, which needed sorting. I realised that I would have to make a move before the situation got out of hand, but deep down I resented the fact that Paul was relinquishing responsibility. Actually, I felt quite reluctant to take the initiative so late at night; equally, neither Paul nor I wanted confrontation.

But however reluctantly, I decided to move out into the cold night air and with the sea breeze getting under my light clothing, I approached Joe in quite a deliberate manner. Paul waited. He knew without any doubt that I was making a move on behalf of the whole team.

"Are you prepared to do extra shifts with the driving, Joe?"

"I'll do whatever you want, but I am not having that maniac

in the same wagon as me!" Without compromise, Joe was clear about his agenda. He knew what he was not going to do and, still trying to make his point, he was by now pacing back and forth, stamping his feet.

"OK, fair enough. This, then, is what we'll do." Wiping some sea spray away from my face I turned to Freddie. "OK Freddie, you have a choice, either I will drive you back to the motorway, then you can hitch a lift back, or you can come for the ride as a passenger/navigator. The choice is yours, but, what we were not going to do is have you going over the top every time a difficult situation arises, and insisting on blaming everybody else."

Recognising that I had sussed his game, he immediately flipped into a rage, hurling abuse at me for all he was worth... on and on.

"No more words Freddie! Cool it! Make your choices!" Paul knew I would not be moved or manipulated by Freddie's temper tantrums or his threats. I was far too long in the tooth to buckle under that sort of pressure.

"I'll do my fair share of driving. We'll take shifts, two on, one off...all the way." With that, I simply turned away. Subject closed. I already knew what Freddie would do.

As usual my husband began to soften his stance. He already felt sorry for Freddie and having experienced me in these situations before, knew I would be unrelenting as I was not planning on taking chances.

We all eventually boarded the ferry with Freddie, now uneasily keeping a low profile. The excitement of being with the other 240 drivers saved the day and broke the strained atmosphere.

By morning the only thing on our minds was adjusting to right hand driving through France's rush hour traffic. Joe and I drove the first leg in our respective vehicles, Joe leading the way.

Paul soon realised Joe was setting a much harder and faster

pace than I would be prepared to drive, so we had to devise a system of communication signals: three flashes on the brake or headlights meant an emergency, two flashes meant slow down.

Within an hour, all the 120 wagons had spread out across France and it soon became heart warming to see another truck with the 'Convoy of Hope' Red Heart sticker on the side. This, after all, reassured us we were still following the correct route.

We had no map, only a written itinerary, as stupidly we had presumed to think that the whole convoy would be travelling together. It was amazing how two day's later we all managed to finish in Zagreb, Croatia a thousand miles further on, and all within a few hours of each other.

As the next two days passed, I was learning to 'rough it' for the first time in my fifty-two years of life! I became quite accustomed to sleeping across the vehicle's front seats, trying to nurse a still fresh fourteen inch stomach wound, whilst the gear lever seemed to stick into every conceivable tender part of my body. Paul realising that this journey was not too much fun, and along with sleep depravation, he knew that the conditions would do little to sweeten my already stretched disposition towards Freddie.

"I suppose staying in anything less than a five star hotel is your idea of sleeping rough!" he teased. He knew it was wise to give me a wide berth and it would only take Freddie's negative responses, coupled with my tiredness and 'Old Spiky' would have a hey-day. We both knew my weakness and would be careful not to give 'Old Spiky' the opportunity.

By now we were sure Freddie had some deep psychological problem, so we were all quite determined to be pleasant and supportive towards him, and were certainly prepared to be as kind as possible. During each change over of drivers, the question was always, who will travel with Freddie?

With my logic, I suggested Paul, as he had the kindest disposition in the team. I elected him as the safest companion. At least, that was my theory until we arrived at the Austrian border when, to my absolute amazement, Paul came running over.

"I have a deep desire just to stop Freddie's continual insinuations and innuendoes. It's like he is determined to cause friction. Do I have your permission to punch this guy right on the end of his nose?" he pleaded.

"Absolutely, categorically NO!" I replied in one of my typically authoritative voices which says… I'm not joking!

"He's driving my crazy! I can't stand any more of him. I've done everything, prayed and praised and still he eats away at me."

"Come on Paul, we are 'Christians' and would you believe, Christians just don't do things like that!" Paul could see I was trying hard not to laugh, and at the same time trying to deflect his growing frustration.

"OK, you're right," he agreed, determinedly planting a quick kiss on the end of my nose and he returned quite happily to his vehicle.

I was sitting back, reflecting on Paul's unusual response, when suddenly, Joe approached the wagon quite heated, and to my amazement with the words. "Paul's just been arrested! He's had to go with the border guards."

I gulped whilst Joe was telling his story. Joe's words were coming in quick succession.

"We were going through passport control when Freddie let out such a mouthful of stuff about you. Paul gave him a warning signal, which Freddie just completely ignored. Then, I couldn't believe it! Paul just simply picked him up by the front of his clothes and…"

At that moment I noticed Freddie peeping round the corner of a wall, his facial expression smirking, fully triumphant. He had finally found, and pressed, Paul's red button. I felt sick inside. I knew Paul's loss of control would hurt him a lot more than it would Freddie. In Freddie's sick way of thinking he could now glory in being the victim and feel justified in saying, "Look at what those so called Christians have done to me."

Thankfully, Paul's so-called arrest only came to a mild warning, and by this time feeling quite ashamed, and not wishing to be beaten by Freddie's cruel sense of injustice, Paul suggested they both try again. However it was in Slovenia when we were hopelessly lost that Freddie started to goad Paul again.

The now familiar tones of 'This is your fault. Look what you've done' sent shivers down my spine. He was gnawing away at Paul like a dog with a bone, still pushing him to his limits. Freddie seemed to have no awareness that maybe; just maybe, he was contributing to his own difficulties and that of the team in some small way.

Personally, I was amazed how Paul just kept turning away; I certainly had to wrestle with some inward desires myself. However, instead of reacting, as one might expect under such provocation, Paul just decided to pray in tongues out loud. Freddie couldn't understand what was happening and, when we inadvertently managed to get on the right road, Freddie exclaimed he had just seen a miracle. We all nodded our head in unbelief. The real miracle was Paul had been given the grace to respond gently.

Soon after this event, one of the other drivers, a Catholic Priest, reversed over a tree trunk whilst parking. Much to his dismay, he had lost his reverse gearing. On hearing from Freddie about the so called miracle of finding our way, the lovely priest approached smiling, and asked, half-joking, half-serious, but definitely tongue in cheek. "Do you think you people could have a word upstairs about my gearbox?"

CHAPTER 2

Our People Are Dying

It's quite a sight seeing 120 vehicles of all shapes and sizes and all wearing red hearts emblazoned with the words 'Convoy of Hope' stretching along a dual carriageway. Our team was about number twenty-four in the line, and as we looked back from a bend in the road, we could see a two-mile line of 'love on the move.'

"Isn't it a privilege to be part of such a gigantic outreach to our fellow man?" I commented excitedly, proud of the love demonstrated by the sacrificial giving of the folks back home. There was a very real sense of 'the cavalry coming to the rescue,' and our real expectation was to deliver food and other items directly into the hands of refugees who were most in need.

In Zagreb we were all led into a large compound, where all the large industrial units were surrounded by a six foot high steel fence. All the vehicles were eventually parked neatly in rows and the drivers were formed into groups for photographs. The media wished to maximise the arrival of such a large convoy of private individuals.

That evening, as was the custom, everyone was graciously entertained by a choir of fresh-faced youngsters, and though the general feeling was that we hadn't come to be entertained, we were appreciative of the kindness shown to us. Freddie, thankfully, had used the social atmosphere to join with another group of unsuspecting travellers and our team gratefully breathed sighs of relief.

It was announced that the convoy would, the following day, be split up into smaller groups, going to various districts and different refugee camps. Some vehicles were required to travel to the most dangerous areas, and the team was disappointed when we were not chosen.

"Maybe they think women shouldn't be sent to unsafe areas," Paul commented ruefully. He knew this would not satisfy his 'little woman' for long!

That evening, having been booked into a hotel in the centre of Zagreb for a mere ten pounds sterling, we had our first sight of beds and showers for days. Naturally we all relished the thought of a nice hot shower followed by a good night's sleep. With the lifts not working Paul and I trudged to the fifth floor looking forward to a time of personal space and reflection. On finding our room Paul took a full-length dive onto the hard single bed as I made my way straight to the bathroom. Sinking into the bed covers, Paul was about to enjoy a few minutes peace so was naturally reluctant to respond to my plaintive cries which I delivered from the bathroom.

"Oh no Paul, I can't believe it. No hot water!" I squawked through my chattering teeth. I was, by this time, already stripped off and freezing in the cold dank shower cubicle.

"Please bring me that phone and a towel." It only took a few moments on the phone for this shivering wreck to find and use some remnant of femininity as I called some of the other male drivers billeted on the fourth floor.

"Hi you guys. Have you got any hot water on your floor?" I waited with bated breath for their positive response. "Then please keep your eyes closed, we are on our way!" This was no time for false modesty. At a time like this a girl has to do what a girl has to do. Paul and I grasped the opportunity of the pleasure of a hot shower together. It was an even greater pleasure later for me to have a warm husband cocooned around me like an electric blanket. We were not blind to the fact that we were one of the convoy's few husband and wife teams, so on this occasion it was a privilege we weren't slow to enjoy.

The following day, after an early breakfast, we were back on duty in the compound champing at the bit, eager to be off. As each small group left, blaring horns accompanied each intrepid pioneer. We noticed that the Catholic priest had no personal food for the journey, so with a mischievous glimpse across to Paul first, I asked. "No packed food sir? Maybe you thought God would provide? Well maybe He has." I smiled, and patted him on the shoulder for good measure in my new role of tarnished angel, as I gave him a couple of bars of chocolate.

At last it was our turn to leave and we all felt we were finally going to be able to do something positive to help the victims of this crazy war. We were destined for an area about twenty miles outside Zagreb called Petrina and we all set off feeling quite upbeat. Two vans plus two other cars with trailers, made our small convoy up to six. We had no difficulty in finding our destination but were amazed when we eventually found ourselves being shown to a double garage adjacent to a smallholding, where we were asked to unload.

The family directing operations were most welcoming and assured us these goods would be used to feed refugees in the area. "Hey, wait a moment," I interjected. Whilst we had no reason not to trust the family, we had difficulty in hiding our disappointment at not meeting with and feeding people directly. It was the only way we would know if the food would be given *freely* to those for whom it was intended, and not sold on the black market. However much I tried to be positive, I sensed that there was some other agenda in operation. I could not come to terms with the request to unload into a storehouse, with no understanding, or proof as to what would happen to the food next. What did we need to find out? I started to probe further.

"Where exactly are the refugees at present?" We all felt we needed answers, whist trying not to insult the family in question. The family was most gracious with their responses. Their sixteen-year-old son made a few phone calls to the local army and it was decided our whole group could be taken further inland.

The family drove their car in front, and led us for about four miles until we reached a steep riverbank where the brown mud somehow supported a pontoon bridge. Apparently I was expected to drive across the choppy waters along two eighteen-inch metal tracks. Immediately Paul jumped out to help in the guiding process, clearly confident that I could handle our vehicle.

A van with a trailer was in front, so I told myself '*if he can negotiate this bridge with a trailer on the back, then of course I can.*' I took heart in the fact that at least Paul thought I could manage. The van in front skidded from side to side, its back wheels spinning in the soft brown mud as it sunk further and further into the quagmire. The whole exercise was a near impossibility, but at the third attempt, somehow the van driver successfully negotiated his way out and across the bridge and up the steep, muddy bank on the far side.

Now it was my turn! Paul was by this time on the bank guiding the wheels of our vehicles with frantic hand signals, maybe now, not quite so confident in my driving skills. I fixed my gaze on him. A big cheer went up when, much to Paul's delight, his 'little woman' managed to negotiate the crossing at the first attempt. I thought of Dean, who had been my P.A when I was last in business back home:

'*This is just the sort of stuff that boys all together enjoy, so why was I there instead of him?*' After all, this gave an adrenalin rush with little danger; but, '*Lord, where are the people that we've come to serve?*'

Eventually we stopped outside another old family house, and it was decided this was the end of the line and we could all unload our gifts into their garage. Somehow, something was still not fitting into place; none of the team had peace within. Would leaving the food here honour the people who had given it back home? Why did our guide think this garage would be any better than the last? Still we had no guarantees as to where the food would finish up.

We could see locals gathering in the distance, pushing and shoving. The sense of mounting tension and aggression indicated to me that we were at least moving in the right direction. But maybe we hadn't yet arrived at the area of greatest need? A heated discussion arose between the self-appointed leaders. We stood back and observed like flies on a wall. My questions would not go away, "Who is going to get this food? Where are the really needy people and what is the extent of their need?"

Amidst all the confusion of the unloading with which the others were occupied, one of the locals in a thirty-five year-old Austin Somerset pick-up truck beckoned Paul to follow him with our vehicle. Maybe now we could quietly slip away unnoticed.

The guide beckoned again and pointed to some woods about two miles ahead. Mist was hanging in the sultry air and I experienced a strange sensation running up and down my spine.

"Serb front lines," Paul commented, to give me a chance to change my mind. I simply gave him a sweet smile trying to ignore the rapid rise and fall of my chest as my heart began to pound frantically.

We continued in blind faith, following a stranger down pot holed narrow lanes, in a strange country, and where we were exposed for the first time to the devastation left by war. Man's hatred and greed had raped and burnt-out homes. Evil had blown apart families, destroyed them and their homes in seconds. An old thick-walled type house had a huge, jagged hole in the gable-end, exposing the remains of children's posters on their bedroom walls. The rest of the house contents had long since been burnt or stolen. Such extraordinary sights had an air of normality, which we found absolutely chilling.

The devastation indicated we were now on the right track to serve, and our apprehension increased as we drove closer to the threatening woods. "Paul, do you realise we are now well within the sight of snipers?" I was testing his awareness. He simply smiled, patted me on the knee and kept his foot well down on the accelerator. I felt as secure as I could under the circumstances, given we were in uncharted territory.

After making a right hand turn we came upon a dirt track path leading to a farmyard. We stopped, simply because we couldn't go any further, many local residents soon gathered. These people, who had been carrying out their everyday tasks collecting wood, feeding chickens, now gathered silently and stood uneasily around our van. Nearly all the women were wearing black. Neither they, nor we knew what to expect. I could see that in these circumstances my blonde hair must have made me seem like an alien from outer space. Thirty or forty people congregated and it was not long before, much to Paul's delight, the men were inviting us to share some home-made vino. These smiling, yet weather worn-faced people were looking to give.

The women seemed old and most of them were wearing cut down men's shoes, all very worn and mostly held on by string. Thankfully that was something with which we knew we could offer some real help. The women quite understandably were pushing and shoving trying to get as near to the vehicle's now open back door as possible. First out of the box was a pair of shoes ideal for a little girl. I looked around. There were quite a few children so we sorted out all the children's shoes we could find and passed them to the rear of the crowd to enable the little ones to be fitted first.

One of the younger women held a very attractive, black velvet slipper and was beckoning for the other. Paul pulled the complete box out of the van and in seconds, in a frenzied air of desperation, the crowd devoured about fifty pairs of shoes. Next Paul produced a big box of sugar and started to hand out individual packets to the heaving mass of battling women.

The men seemed to be holding back, apparently quite used to the women doing women's work in the situation, as Paul passed food out as quickly as he could. No sooner had an item come into the open air, than there were about six pairs of hands trying to grab it.

The pressure in front of us was growing, and Paul realised the frenzy in front of us was becoming ugly; someone could get hurt. Paul must have sensed I felt quite vulnerable and we were both relieved to find the next box contained a large box of chocolate bars all wrapped in Christmas paper as little presents. Immediately, as Paul handed out the bars as quickly as possible, the atmosphere changed. The women started to laugh, Paul and I began to laugh and even the men at the back joined in. Soon we were sharing the very joy that we had come to bring! Paul knew I would not have missed these moments for all the five star hotels in the world!

Pulling out a jar of expensive face cream I laughingly mimed what it was. One younger woman nudged my arm. "Please," she pleaded. I knew that jar of cream would have been like gold dust if I had I been in the young woman's shoes. It was a pleasure to give. After distributing goods for over two hours we finally surveyed the empty cardboard boxes and paper strewn over the now disorderly farmyard.

We were tidying up when to my dismay, I noticed the young woman, still standing with the one black, velvet slipper in her hand. Frantically Paul and I searched but did not find its partner. I knew from experience what she would be feeling. It was as if Father Christmas had just come and given her an empty box.

In that moment I remembered how as a young child I had pretended to be asleep under the bedclothes in my old black iron bed on Christmas Eve. My father and brother came in and out of my room several times, filling a pillowcase and my mind with words of "Oh, she will love this," or "this will taste good." The next morning what my imagination perceived as wonderful presents from Santa soon turned out to be cabbage, dirty old potatoes and a few oranges thrown in for good measure. It was awful to realise that now we could be the instruments of further pain for these people and not the pleasure we had intended.

By late afternoon we were forced to think of the rest of the convoy, and how the others would be feeling about our subtle disappearance. Reluctantly we bade our farewells with an extra hug for the young woman with the 'half gift' resolving to do better next time and as an after thought, I went to the cab, brought out my shoes, so glad to be able to uphold the name of Jesus.

We all hugged each other again, waving goodbye, realising we had received much more than we could ever have given. We were in fact so filled with joy that we had no fear as we drove past the woods on the way back.

It was understandable when we found the others, including Joe, hopping with frustration. Arrangements had been made for an army lorry to take the whole group further into the area, which had been under attack, and Paul and I were delaying their departure. Thankfully there was no time to discuss the situation and the entire group hurriedly piled into the back of the camouflaged lorry as Paul and I tried to keep a low profile.

It nearly took a crane to get me on board and for the first time, I probably showed my age and condition. To ease the pain in my back and stomach I crouched down, perched on my heels and used my knees as a spring board to counteract the effects of the continual bumping as the heavy lorry travelled over the rough ground

"You should be at home taking it easy," Paul encouraged – just a little too late!

"Taking it easy! What's that? Come on Paul, you know me better than that. We all have identical suitcases; it's just that some of us pack a little more in than others."

The lorry continued over rough dirt tracks; through an area where every home had been shelled, sprayed with bullets and then left to burn out, exposing the devastating effects of the evil engulfing a whole community. This awful sight is scored into our memories forever. These families had their women raped; their lives and children hacked to pieces. I wondered how victims of man's desire for power and greed live with these scars. Could the people who had laughed over the chocolate bars have suffered similar experiences or indeed perpetrated them?

I was beginning to understand just a little and wanted to put my arms around these people as a nation, hold them and somehow be the very channel through which they could receive healing.

"Put that camera away, you idiot!" shouted one of the drivers.

I was shaken out of my thoughts. The lorry stopped abruptly. Half the group were acting as if this was a guided tour around central London.

I found the anger well up inside me. *'How dare we come and take photographs of these people as if they are exhibits in a zoo? And how dare we come here with left over clothing with buttons missing?'* Then it hit me like a sledgehammer. *'How dare we come here to get a pay off... of a feel good factor!'*

I wanted to lash out, but at the same time I was also deeply embarrassed. It seemed to me, we were piling insult upon injury. I felt alone, as if I was the only one seeing. It was isolating, yet I questioned, *'How dare I think I am the only one to feel all these emotions?'*

Again, I was wrenched sharply away from my internal struggle.

"Be careful where you walk! There could be landmines!" called the driver.

"Come on," I suggested, eager to get us amateurs out of there before we insulted these people further. I felt sick within. *'Who do we think we are anyway? What do we think we are doing coming here to look at the sights?'* I felt a sense of deep shame and embarrassment. I had finally got in touch with the hidden agenda I had sensed earlier; 'the feel good factor' That's it, we have done our bit, we have got the 'feel good about ourselves' factor. So now it gives us the right to take our photographs and go home to show how brave we have been. Screaming inside I banged the air with my fist. How dare we? How dare we? I looked around wondering what the others were seeing and how they were reacting.

One of the men's trailers was still full with aid, so we decided to stop again in the village on the way back. We off-loaded at one of the local homes and within a short space of time; people were streaming from all over, as if summoned by a Heavenly Call. The aid looked impressive. There were commercial sized packets of soap powder, boxes of cereal, which looked more like pan scrubbers than food, and many tins of baby milk. When we reached the stage for the clothes to be unpacked, I did my best to hide a white straight skirt that would have looked wonderful on Princess Grace of Monaco, but was not really suitable for these ladies. It brought home to me how little I had previously understood the plight of these people and that there were many people who were still unaware of the reality of the situation in Croatia at that time.

Thankfully, before I blew a fuse, my attention was diverted as the host of the house beckoned us all inside for some welcome refreshments. The kitchen/living room was quite large and lives revolved round the black, wood burning, cooking stove. The whole team was hungry and quite worn out by this time.

Small children looking tired were whining around their mother's skirt, whilst we looked at the hard, abrasive, brown cereal. It was then I realised the mother didn't know what this cereal was, or what to do with it. Standing up and quietly moving towards the kitchen stove, I found a burnt saucepan, mixed some of the baby milk with water and put it on the stove to warm. Placing two brown squares in two dishes with spoons full of sugar; I carefully poured on the improvised milk. The two children eagerly took the bowls, and moved onto the settee next to Paul for some comfort.

Somehow I managed to communicate to the mother, "Now, tomorrow you show the other mothers what to do." The mother smiled. What joy! At last I personally had been useful. Now, I was more than ready for bed. "Come on you men. Please could we crawl back into our own little foxholes?"

In the compound, the next day started exceptionally cold and very damp. However, a brief meeting this day would change the course of our lives forever. Ninety-nine percent of the large original convoy had already left for England and Paul and I were about to leave, when one of the other drivers came running over.

"There are two men at the metal fence and it looks as if they're trying to attract your attention," he panted.

Tentatively I followed Paul over to the fence to see what the men wanted. Immediately we came face to face with a young boy about fifteen years of age. He had a lovely facial bone-structure, beautiful teeth with a winning smile. The other man was about thirty-eight years old and had a kind and gentle face.

Both were shivering with the cold as they were wearing light summer clothing, which, although of good quality, was little protection against the now falling snow. The young boy spoke in broken English.

"My name is Deni. You…please…help us! We need food. Medical Aid! Our town… Breza in Bosnia."

"Bosnia? Where is Bosnia? Isn't there a war going on there or something? How far?" I enquired, wishing I had paid more attention in the geography class at school.

The tears, either from the cold or emotion, ran down the young man's face. Paul looked over to the car, which was parked nearby. "Fairly new! How come they need help?" I was following his train of thought. We were both trying to rationalise what we were seeing with what we were being asked.

"Paul, could you call the lady from the UN over, and ask her to get an interpreter."

The young boy was quickly writing phone numbers on a small piece of grubby paper and desperately pushing it at us through the fence. Again, I searched his face. He tried to explain.

"Please help us. Our people are dying! You don't understand. Please, will you come?"

We were empty and it would take us three weeks to go back to England and return with food. That's assuming we knew where Breza in Bosnia was, and would it be safe?

"Haven't you got a war going on or something?" I blurted out trying to rationalise all the thoughts in my mind.

"It's OK, my Father, many soldiers, my Father will protect you."

"Stop. Stop. Your Father protect us, I think not. If anyone is going to protect us, I prefer it be our heavenly Father, bless you… thank you…and we don't even know where Bosnia is," I kept protesting trying to search my instincts, by which time the cold was biting hard. The two men seemed desperate. But one thing was for sure, this boy was deadly serious.

At last the lady from the UN arrived bringing an interpreter to help in communication. We watched attentively as the conversation became more and more heated. This boy really was desperate for help for his people. By now my senses were working over-time.

Now turning towards us and looking us firmly in the eyes, the UN lady was ready to give her advice. "Forget it, you two. Go back to England. It's not safe. It's a job for the Army. I'll pass on the need to Brussels. You would just get hi-jacked."

My computer brain did a quick re-take. *'Many soldiers, my father will protect you. Hi-jacked? Not safe? How did we know whom to believe? Who should we trust?'* Confused and helpless I turned to Paul. "Can we give them your new jumpers from the van?" Paul was quick to respond, fetching over his new, red birthday present for one of them. "Lord, what do you want us to do? We want to help, but I just couldn't see how."

I tuned into my inner voice. *'Pray with them?'* At first I tried to ignore the inner lead thinking maybe I was imagining things. I was not good at this praying for strangers bit. But if I wanted answers then I had better listen… and what is more… obey.

"Please." I hesitated. "Could we pray with you?" The men agreed somewhat apprehensively as we all held hands through the cold, wire fencing. The wind was biting. The men were blue in the face although looking a little more comfortable in their new English sweaters.

We prayed simply, asking for help and wisdom to know what to do to help these cold souls. They could be genuine. It didn't have to be a trap, but if it was, we certainly could get hi-jacked or worse.

"Lord, we desperately need to know what you want before we make a decision so please direct our path." Suddenly, Paul became aware of the tooting of horns. The others were impatient to set off back to England. Reaching again through the wire fence to shake hands, we bid farewell, not making any commitment, other than, "We'll see what we can do."

A few days later in England, I bombarded my long-suffering husband with endless questions.

"Was it not Martin Luther King who said, 'I have a dream?' Paul, is killing ever justified? Where would we stand if an aggressor came to the door of our home or country? Do we have the right to try and stop them?" Now, raising my voice, "What would have happened to us, in the 1939/45 war if others had not been prepared to die for our freedom?" Paul gave no answer, for he knew from experience, I was about to go through one of my soul-searching exercises. He had seen me wrestle many times before, and knew I would have to find my own way out of this uncharted territory. Were there answers in the pit I was digging?

One part of me was asking: '*What are we doing in this country? Have we completely stopped refugees coming here for safety? It seems that you cannot enter our country without a visa. But, you cannot get a visa in Bosnia either.*'

What a contradiction? My frustration was growing. The labour pains had started. I knew in my heart that we were blessed to live in a country which at least tries to protect those fleeing persecution, torture and degrading treatment. After all, isn't our country second only to Germany with such a large number of people asking for protection from persecution in their home-countries?

'So why does our country close the door now with war in Europe?' I reasoned for myself.

'I suppose we would sink down to Australia with the weight of millions of immigrants if we didn't. Paul, what would Jesus do?'

A few days later he found me sitting in my study staring at a copy of the UN Universal Declaration of Human Rights. Although Paul knew I was not willing to get involved in politics, he also knew I needed to make up my own mind about certain issues for which I had more questions than answers.

"Paul listen to this. Paragraph thirteen states. 'Everyone has the right to leave any country, including his own and return to his country.' And what's more," I went on getting quite excited, "paragraph fourteen states: 'Everyone has the right to seek and to enjoy in other countries, asylum from persecution.' Surely, this must be as God intended it to be?"

Message to the World

Do you out there, well fed, and sleek,
know what it is, when there is no sleep?
Do you REALLY care that I'm unfed?
That I couldn't find my dad, and Mother's dead?
They torched my home – how could it be –
'They' were the friends who came to tea?
Each cruel night the cold wind bites,
while they admire their Christmas lights.
What Christmas present waits for me?
Just a sniper's bullet – that will set me free.
Who will help in my misery?

Written by Ron Kaye in 1993 at the height of the Balkan conflict, and given to the couple on their return to England. This poem has been slightly changed in 2012 in view of the historical facts.

CHAPTER 3

The Call

Why is it my greatest adventures in life always start with an argument with God? *'No Lord, you don't really want us to go to Bosnia do you? Not me Lord. It'll be so cold!'* I knew 'He' always manages to touch my heartstrings whenever 'He' wanted to, and 'He' always wins! *'There are times, Lord, when you just don't play fair,'* I complained as I had one of my inner battles again.

It was about two weeks before Christmas. Paul and I were doing our family shopping, having just returned from our 'one off trip' to Croatia. We stood motionless at the checkout as the till rang up £94 I took a deep breath, looked at Paul, knowing we only had about £86 to our names in the bank.

As we walked out of the shop with our parcels, I stood on the pavement confronting my poor husband with full force. "What are we doing? We are spending money which we haven't got, to give to people here in England who don't need it, and those two men at that metal fence in Zagreb, are still trying to get help for starving people! Paul, what are we doing?"

Another argument upstairs. I was aware that I was being moved within my spirit in a way that didn't make any sense to me. Within days and with no inner peace but wishing to make sure I was not just being an emotional female, I decided to share my thoughts with our Church on Sunday and ask if any person felt a leading in the matter.

After the service a young woman approached us very tentatively. "I don't know if this will help, but I will tell you what we were told some years ago." The young woman spoke now with authority. "When Jesus said, 'Go into all the world and take the Gospel message.' He actually didn't say anything about coming back."

"That's it! That's it!" I nearly jumped out of my skin. It was just as if the light had come on. I could hardly believe my own clarity in the situation. "Of course! He said go! So, as long as we are prepared to be obedient and go, that's all that matters. We are called to be obedient and trust Him for the rest."

Now there was such a surge of energy I could hardly contain myself. "OK, Lord, I'm not a doctor. I can't save lives, but we can do whatever you ask of us. You lead, and we will follow." I searched my dear husband's face for confirmation. "We don't know what He will have in store for us in Bosnia, but if we are willing, I am sure God himself will provide all we need; food, transport and funds within the week, then we could be there on Christmas Day. That has to be the safest day to travel into Bosnia," I reasoned in some sort of illogical way, and as if an after thought added, "and please Lord, give us the grace and courage to follow."

Within a few days on faith, we had funds and enough food aid to fill the van, which we planned to hire for the journey. We approached the counter with the agreed hire charge in Paul's pocket in cash. The lady behind the counter smiled.

"There is an extra insurance premium that will need paying… £245 please," she said. We stood like children in total embarrassment.

"Oh! Wait a minute, what did you say your name was? This must be for you," said the lady behind the counter. "Some gentleman heard you speak about Bosnia on the radio and phoned us earlier. He paid £75 off your account with his credit card." Wow, we quietly smiled towards Heaven, is this what walking in God's will is all about?

A few days later in our Yorkshire home sat the wife of Emir, a refugee who was still in central Bosnia. She was a young attractive lady with two well-behaved young sons. Not only did she care for her own two children but she mothered her four-year-old niece, Nela. One dreadful night, all the civilians in their small town came under attack when the whole area was besieged by tanks and battle crazed soldiers. Their home and those of all their immediate neighbours were beginning to burn fiercely, when the mother in a moment of immense terror jumped out of the back bedroom window into an immediate burst of gunfire which reverberated around the whole area. Because of the flames, Fuad, the father, hurled out the child and quickly followed in a desperate leap himself. Again, blasts of gunfire. A life and death confrontation, all in sacred last moments.

The young mother's barely warm body lay dead in the cold night air. Fuad lay bleeding; shot in the chest. Mercifully, the child was still breathing and alive. Only nine of their immediate neighbours survived that night. The rest were either mown down by gunfire, or burnt to death.

Neighbours later rescued Fuad and Nela and when we eventually met this child in England, she would sit happily on my lap allowing me to gently comb her dark, curly hair. In turn she would delight in combing my fine, straight hair. Together we were wrapped up in a special place of tenderness where we could share a deep trust without words.

Now here we were in our home with Emir's wife, she was sharing the story of how her husband had been sick in hospital at the early stages of the war. She managed to escape to England with her two children and the young Nela.

Since the British Government had ordered a halt to all refugees from Bosnia without visas entering England, they, like many other families had become separated and were desperate in their need to be together. Emir could not come to England without a visa. He could not obtain a visa in central Bosnia because he had no passport and there was no British Embassy in wartime Bosnia. It seemed our government had forgotten that when people fled their homes in nights of terror, they did not stop to pick up their passports.

Many families were simply separated through no fault of their own. Emir's wife had come to us and nervously asked if a letter could be delivered to her husband, somewhere in Zenica. I looked at her compassionately and promised that if, by some miracle we managed to find this one man out of the thousands of refugees, then the wife could be sure, not only would we give him the letter, but a big hug from her as well.

We had been warned about the risk of carrying anything exclusively for any particular ethnic group in the political climate, but if a moment's pleasure and some hope could be given to this couple, then in my book it was worth the risk.

*****

Travelling south in England in winter with black ice on the roads, was no small nights work, but we managed to catch the 4.30am ferry. After compiling paperwork, driving through France, Belgium and into Germany, my fatigue was getting the better of me and I was beginning to nag Paul unmercifully. Why was it so difficult for him to hear my need for rest after thirty-six hours of travel?

The pain in my back and neck had increased beyond the level of my tolerance. I was well past my sell by date, and the limits of my endurance had by this time well surpassed my patience with Paul's blindness. It had always seemed to me the more I was prepared to endure, the more the men in my life seemed to expect.

'*When will they hear or see my needs?*' was my inner cry. It seemed to me that there were many things Paul and I needed to agree on if we were going to survive as a couple within this new chapter of our lives.

Other than the grace of God the problem within my spine is there permanently, but at times of self-neglect the pain comes into full focus. At that moment it only takes someone asking the same question three times for my patience to fail, and yes, I blow again like an old steam engine. So was it surprising Paul was about to get another verbal backlash if he didn't stop the vehicle soon?

Paul and I knew very little about the current fighting or the political situation in Bosnia. Our only lead to re-connecting with the young stranger we had met for a few minutes at a metal fence previously in Zagreb, was a phone number quickly scribbled on a crumpled piece of paper. However despite my lack of grace, yet with child-like trust and in simple faith, now in Germany we made the call.

*****

"Deni? No, Deni school!" replied the female voice on the other end of the phone.

"OK, I phone tonight." Automatically getting into broken English, as it wasn't difficult to realise the person at the other end of the phone could only understand a little of the English language.

That evening whilst I was still struggling to find sleep, Paul phoned again and arranged for us to meet Deni at 8am on Christmas morning at the same six-foot metal fence in Zagreb where we had previously met him a few weeks before, this being the only place we knew.

Paul and I had not yet discovered anything about the mountains of paperwork needed to get through the Balkan Bureaucracy. We were relying only on our passports to get us through borders, with a lot of expected help from 'the heavenly realm'. Without that extra dimension, contemplating this journey would have been totally unrealistic at the best of times, let alone in winter wartime.

After a lot of negotiating at customs we managed by some miracle to get through the Croatian border on Christmas morning. The temperature was below zero and a light covering of snow fell as we waited in Zagreb excitedly anticipating the look on the young man's face when he saw all we had brought for his people.

Being Christmas day the whole area had an uncanny feel about it. There were only a few cars on the roads and of course no buses. It had not occurred to us that Deni would have to walk several miles to make the rendezvous.

"Look, he's coming!" I said excitedly.

In the distance we could see the tall frame of a good looking young man, who was red in the face from his long walk in the biting winds. He almost danced up to us. His broad smile and the spontaneous hugs we exchanged soon put us all at ease.

Deni was soon on board navigating us out of Zagreb past the majestic old buildings but in a moment of irritation, whilst trying to negotiate the vehicle through a complicated one way traffic system, I let rip with, "Oh! For goodness sake Paul, do shut up!"

Immediately there was a roar of laughter. "You like Basil Faulty and Sybil! from the television programme." Well, I suppose that's one way of looking at us as a couple.

I was pleased this young man could find some humorous way of handling being in our company. We have discovered over the years, that some people have needed to adjust their own expectations when they experience being around us. When Paul and I interact we are unwilling to play the game of 'perfect people.' As a form of sport, Paul can't resist winding me up in a playful way, I give a warning signal, which he invariably misses or chooses to ignore. The winding up game continues. I bite back. Paul goes into victim mode... so again I get to be the baddie. We have tried to adjust our interaction over the years but I am clear, we all need people around us who are prepared to love us as we are and not judge us from their own expectations. So I was pleased that this young man could be so open in his responses. It wasn't long until I found myself comparing him with my own sixteen-year-old son at home, Richard.

As the journey progressed, Deni started to try to explain the war and began to tell us about some of the horrific stories of brutal killings and repeated rapes. What a stark contrast there was between this boy's life and Richard's.

Apparently it had been Deni's father, Meho, who had instigated the two men coming to the fence for help in Zagreb which initiated our original meeting. Now, after a fourteen-hour drive over snow covered mountain roads, Paul and I had arrived at a flat in Split, where we were about to be introduced to the man himself.

Although Paul and I were exhausted, these Europeans seemed to come to life at night! A meal was hastily prepared and we had the opportunity to unwind. Only Deni spoke any English, making it difficult for any of us to communicate at all verbally, so now we had to use all our other senses to help us learn how to build some bridges of understanding.

Deni's father was a very charismatic man, with so much presence which seemed to flow out of his very pores. I was not surprised he had such a good looking son and wondered what his mother was like.

It turned out Meho was a Muslim and Deni's mother was a Croat, now living with Deni in Zagreb for safety. The family had previously lived in Sarajevo and owned another weekend house by the sea. Meho had a factory in Sarajevo and each time I asked what he did, the reply came, "business man."

"We are all 'business men" I came back at him. "The question is whose business are we about?" Quite understandably, it seemed there was only one business for Meho at this time and that was that of survival of his family and his country.

His older son, Mirza, had been sent to America at the start of the war and was now at university studying to be a doctor. Meho wasted no time showing us press cuttings about Mirza. He was clearly a man who inspired his sons and cared deeply about his people. He explained how his people had to try to defend themselves with their hands tied behind their backs, because of the arms embargo set by NATO.

When he heard our story and realised we were just two ordinary people, who had come in faith, trying only to answer a call for help, he immediately went over to a drawer and produced the most beautiful leather document case from which he extracted a certificate.

"My government has awarded me our country's highest honour, 'The Golden Lily'. After the war is over, we will honour you also." I smiled inwardly thinking that, if we receive our reward on earth, we have no need to receive it in heaven. Aloud I said,

"Thank you, but there is no need," shrugging my shoulders too tired to communicate further.

The following morning there was much discussion about what would happen next, and it was decided Mujo (the older man who had been at the fence with Deni) would accompany us for the rest of the trip into central Bosnia. Mujo was a man with a kind face, a family man with two young children and a wife whom he adored, but I could not get my mind around the situation when I saw this same man pack a revolver into his small bag.

'*What are we getting into?*' I'm sure we both thought, watching apprehensively. I felt a little easier when I saw Meho go past the chair and place a loving hand, authoritatively, on Mujo's shoulder. If it was any consolation to us we were, I was quite sure, in the presence of a great leader.

As if to confirm my thinking as we were leaving, I saw Meho take his son by the shoulders and plant a life time's amount of courage within him with just one firm loving hug. It was a precious moment of immense intimacy and beauty. No wonder this father was the inspiration for his sons.

We drove out of Split, along the coast road, beside the most beautiful of coastlines. The views of the little fishing villages blending into the shimmering deep turquoise waters made us see anew God's gift to mankind.

'*Why? Oh! Why do we work so hard to destroy that which God has given us?*' I cried within.

After many hours of breath taking scenery we turned inland, heading towards Mostar and we were quite unprepared for the abrupt change of mood. Scars of the most brutal cruelty could be seen around every bend. All the roads were pitted with potholes caused by exploding grenades. Every house without exception, as far as the eye could see, was burnt out. Only the broken shells of homes were standing where once on the balconies, amongst the grapevines, families had eaten evening meals in the deep red setting sun.

Amongst the ruins, the odd dog scavenged for food and a few old people walked dejectedly, leading their surviving cow to try to find some grazing. I tried to imagine what it must have been like when tanks fired shells into every home and people tried to flee from the flames, only to be slaughtered by automatic gunfire. The fear! The screams as families saw their loved ones cut down in front of their eyes! The sky alight with the flames dancing silhouetted against the black of night.

'How are these people going to survive? How are they ever going to recover from this?' My mind raced on and on. *'How do we ask them to forgive?'* I reasoned to myself. *'Do we have the right to speak about forgiveness? Given we have not lived through this, how can the bridges of forgiveness and reconciliation be re-built?'*

I was relieved to be distracted when we stopped to buy a few fresh oranges from a seller at the side of the road. Mujo and Deni wanted to take this gift of fresh food for their friends. An old man approached our vehicle and I wound down the van window to give him some chocolate. Deni became very agitated.

"Jacqui, please don't open your window in Bosnia. You don't realise. They can just throw in a grenade!" I was quickly getting the picture, but still felt very much unprepared for our new role. I was very happy that this young man was giving us a crash course on the art of survival.

After pressing on for many hours we passed over the remaining half of a blown up bridge across the Neretva River. The river was a clear, jewel-like turquoise. One could never accurately describe its clarity of colour or the truly magnificent scenery surrounding it. Such beauty only helped to heighten the ugliness of what man was doing to his fellow man.

We proceeded through two tunnels, masonry dangling precariously overhead. I drove carefully being aware of the need to go slowly enough to avoid bringing down any loose concrete, yet fast enough to avoid being too long passing through in the dark.

As we came out the other side we skidded on thick ice, formed by constant drips falling from the long, thin icicles hanging from the craggy, grey rocks. It seemed as if the giant rocks viewing the scenes were themselves crying. I imagined God's heart must have been bleeding also. No wonder He was giving us a heart for these people.

By early evening we were approaching the mountains and Mujo suggested he drive, as the terrain was to become more difficult. I couldn't imagine how, but I let him take control as this was his country and he could find a way through these mountain paths.

The cold night air began to grip as we slowly approached a checkpoint. The local militia came towards my side of the van smiling.

"Dobar Dan," I said putting out a hand and trying my first attempt at this strange language.

"Dobar Dan Lady. English? You cigarettes?"

"Sorry! No!" I searched my mind to see what else I might have to give as a gift. As I was thinking, I saw the guard blow his warm breath into his cold hands.

Paul's gloves lay on the dashboard. "Here, try these. You are going to be cold out there all night." I stretched my hand out through the van window. "Please take them as a gift." Deni and Mujo looked on absolutely bemused. '*Definitely mad*', they must have thought.

"OK, you go through. Good luck!" I smiled but didn't like the, 'good luck' bit.

Why did we need good luck? What's ahead?

Gunfire was heard coming from Sarajevo over to our right. Our route was to the left, over a mountain pass. Mujo was now increasing speed, sensing the impending dark would present new problems.

"We need, go along a smaller road," Deni was explaining, "fighting ahead." The dirt track we turned into was frozen solid and ice was covering it, disguising the eighteen-inch holes we hit every couple of feet, which rocked the van from side to side and then bumped it high into the air. Every time I came back down into the seat pain shot through my spine almost forcing me to shout out, but I was determined not to, the men needed my support not my weakness.

Mujo's eyes darted everywhere. Deni was on Red Alert. I could sense the tension as Paul started to sing, clearly determined not to show any apprehension. The others joined in and this calmed us all as we made our way even deeper into more difficult terrain.

'*There is no way we can get through here,*' I thought, as the van continued to teeter on the edge of the cliff, wheels spinning, then surging forward, up and down all at the same time. This was getting rough! My back and neck were taking unwelcome punishment. There was no way my already damaged back could take this constant banging without the price being paid somewhere in the future. I looked to Paul for re-assurance, but he like most men, seemed to be more comfortable with the safari experience. I was in the minority, so had better keep quiet, after all the only way out was forward.

"We will have to cut across the top of this field. The frozen ruts are just too deep here," advised Deni.

Tracer fire burst across the skyline to our right. The van climbed up at an angle and it was a struggle to keep traction for the wheels on the top edge. As we tried to pass between two old trees, the van's nose was reaching towards the stars. The wheels started to spin as they became lodged in the roots of an old tree. The vehicle sank further down between the hard ruts, and came to rest at an acute angle, its exhaust, by this time, well and truly at the risk of being broken off.

"We'll have to push it," Paul suggested.

"Push it! How are you going to get it out without breaking off the exhaust?" I questioned.

"OK, let's take the load off then we'll be able to get some branches underneath and lift it, hopefully in one piece." I was pleased Paul was listening, it made me feel a lot more secure after all, here we were in a strange land in the middle of a war, 1300 miles from home and if anything happened to the van we were lost. We would have no other way of getting back. My mind was running through the logistics.

Without much enthusiasm for the task in hand, the men started to lift the heavy boxes until the whole area of about fifteen square yards was covered with boxes of every shape and size! None were sealed and, as the occasional one was dropped in haste, it burst open revealing its contents of toilet rolls, sugar and washing powder all packed together.

'*How crazy these things look scattered on the frosty ground in the dark!*' I thought.

The men tried every conceivable way to move our stricken vehicle, but the more they tried the more it skidded in the lightly frozen mud. I wandered a little way away from the activity.

"Lord, we could do with some help. I am going to trust you." I returned to find Paul alone. "Where are the boys?"

Paul replied looking fairly tired and alone amongst the problem. "Gone to get help."

With a quick change of thought pattern, I suggested we had better get some blankets round us. It was well below freezing, and it was going to get worse. I could feel the odd snowflake falling softly on my face.

Silently, I became aware it was Boxing Night. Our friend Jenny in England, had given Paul and I ten pounds each to buy a Christmas present. With unusual wisdom, I had purchased warm hats for us both. Mine was a white, woolly ski-type one which covered all my head and neck, exposing only half my face. Paul's came well over his ears. I snuggled down into the treasured gift and thought about all the family at home. What would they all be doing?

By now the cold was beginning to creep deeper into my bones and I could not feel my feet. The night sky was clear with hundreds of bright stars twinkling in the heavens. We could hear bombs thudding as their shock waves reverberated into the heart of the earth. We could see tracer fire darting across the skyline and home seemed a long way away. I surveyed our position. Dark woods in front; solid, frozen mud behind; more solid mud with rocks to the left and right.

I retreated deeper into my hat to feel again the warmth of Jenny's love. Would there ever be a way back to England?

"Lord I am just going to keep my trust in you but, whatever happens I must just tell the children I love them." I searched for my little tape recorder and as I recorded my message, I heard my own voice trembling with cold and full-blown fear. '*This is quite ridiculous*,' I kept telling myself, as Paul moved towards me and together we walked back along the hedgerow, further away from the white van.

"I want you to know you have been a wonderful wife, and I so love you," my dear husband was saying. Now I knew for sure that he thought we were in real trouble, his loving words did little to calm my fears, but did everything to make the future, whatever happened, OK. I said nothing in response but gently pressed my cheek against his.

"Paul, I can hear voices coming out of the woods! Shush! Be quiet!" The slight rustle from the movement of Paul's anorak sounded like thunder in the still of the cold night air. I mimed to him to drop the white blanket from around his shoulders.

"Let's go to the van," he indicated pointing the way with his hands. I shook my head.

"No. Stay here! Shush!" I beckoned him into the hedgerow. We were about twenty yards from the van when the voices grew louder. "We could get our throats cut for the food we have around that van." At the same time I wondered if Mujo and Deni would ever come back.

Our hearts were thumping as we crouched down closer to the ground, desperately trying to become invisible. The night was still and the light snow and frost glistened. The voices grew even closer. Dark figures loomed out of the woods as if in slow motion. Voices became distinguishable as the people appeared like trees walking towards us.

We each held our breath, our hearts thumping, waiting apprehensively. The tree-like figures headed straight towards the white wagon. It must have seemed as strange as a spaceship from Mars parked there. The men began to poke amongst the open boxes, getting excited and speaking much faster, in a strange tongue, their breath swirling in the ice-cold air.

On the ground, in the moonlight, I could see a large, round, tin of Roses chocolates. Now was my chance! Leaving Paul, I slowly moved forward, speaking so they could hear immediately that I was a woman. Shocked yet unsure, the men looked up.

Hesitantly I moved closer to the tin of chocolates, taking off my gloves as I tried to pick it up. Still smiling and talking I struggled to get the tape off the lid. They waited. What was I trying to do? My fingers were solid with cold and I had to use my teeth to break the tape. Still smiling, I calmly moved in amongst them.

"Help yourselves," I invited, immediately huge hands grabbed the brightly wrapped chocolates. Now everyone was smiling.

Paul appeared as if from nowhere. Thankfully, at that moment, Mujo and Deni also emerged from the woods followed by Chug! Chug! Chug! Could we believe our ears? Yes. It was a tractor brought by the locals to try to pull out the stricken wagon.

The next half-hour was a mixture of men doing what men like to do best in such a situation. Chains were being harnessed round the van's chassis; many men gave instructions while others groped in the boxes to see what they could find.

As I opened a box of food an elderly man was asking, in sign language, if he could have the trousers and thick jumper he had found spilling out from a black polythene bag. I was happy for him to have something warm for himself in return for his assistance and most grateful for the help of all the others. Mujo suggested we give the farmer with the tractor a few Deutsche Marks. This we were pleased to do as we piled the remainder of the Aid back on board.

We waved the tree like figures goodbye, cold and hungry we settled back in the wagon but at least we had the comfort of the working heaters. I wondered how much further we had to travel.

"Oh! Only about another fifty miles, about two or three hours!" Deni said it in a way that indicated it was just up the road. My heart sank, as we were all by this time extremely tired so the prospect was not good news. Tracer fire and shells were still falling in the distance.

'*What are we doing here anyway? How did we get into this stuff?*' I thought with more than a hint of not wanting to play anymore. Fixing my eyes on Deni my heart was again melted by his youthful smile, and I knew why we were here. Although the bumping, rocking and sliding of the van didn't get any easier, we were still much happier to be well on our way, at least until we came to the next checkpoint. Straight away I could see the guards had been drinking, so I decided to keep a low profile.

Mujo spoke with the guards but to no avail. They beckoned for the van papers. As Paul reached into the dashboard for the paperwork, his hand slid back and forth, nothing! There was nothing there! We passed over our passports hoping these would do. The men climbed out of the van and, for about twenty minutes they waved their arms about and bounced words back and forth.

"You go Commander!" Overhearing and, thinking a feminine touch was now needed, I reluctantly moved my weary bones and forced myself into action by sliding across the front seat towards the unshaven leader.

Outside I ran my hands up and down his two-day facial growth and said, as seductively as my pride and husband's presence would allow.

"You naughty man. You've been out with ladies? Tut! Tut! What will your commander say when he sees you, he no pleased!"

He put his arm around my waist; I felt every sinew in my body pull taut but managed a, "come follow me!" as I headed towards the back of the van, searching with my mind and hands to find the bars of chocolate which I knew must be there somewhere.

"For you," I said triumphantly, handing over some chocolate. One of the other soldiers immediately took some bars of goodies uninvited and put them in the inside pocket of his uniform. He seemed satisfied.

To our absolute amazement the guards moved back a couple of paces and allowed us all to move towards the cab.

"Come on! Lads! Let's get out of here before they change their minds!" I said with just a hint of satisfaction, with the result of my performance.

There were no more hold ups that night and we arrived safely but very wearily at our destination. Zenica looked how I had imagined Russia to look. The buildings were all grey and uninteresting, in a state of decay, covered in graffiti. The only grass we could see was worn out, and the area was almost tree-less. An air of total neglect hung everywhere just as if the lifeblood had been wrung out of the town's very heart.

With a combination of tiredness and cold we stood at the entrance of a high block of flats, ten floors high; looking up virtually stunned me into immobility. Staying close together we followed our guides into the darkness. Mujo lit a match, which gave a brief glimpse of the depressing concrete jungle.

"Feel for the banister," urged Paul, as his hand reached out for mine in the dark. "Press your toe against every stair as you climb the steps." We clutched our heavy bags. Eight stairs…five paces… eight more stairs. Then a long walk along the landing to repeat the whole exercise again and again. Where were we going? I gritted my teeth against the darkness and long climb, gripping Paul's hand in the dark.

'*Keep smiling,*' I told myself, '*God knows where we are, even if we don't.*'

There was plenty of light-hearted banter between Paul and the men as we continued to climb to the sixth floor with twelve lots of stairs. As if by magic a light appeared. Silhouetted in the glow from the half-opened door was the round figure of a lady who was already speaking a welcome in an unfamiliar tongue. She reached out a warm hand, which gently wrapped itself around mine, at the same time smiling an inviting welcome. We immediately hugged each other.

Paul and I were home. This was 'a Mummy'. Graciously we were given refreshment as Mummy Nejra, sensing my need, led me to a cramped, but spotlessly clean bathroom. After about three inches of tepid water had been run into the white enamel bath, the water started to run icy cold. Only three inches of water for a bath! Although I did not relish getting undressed in the cold, thereby further exposing my already frozen, tired body, I was grateful for this lady's understanding of my need.

Both Nejra and Edo, the husband, were economists and had worked at the local bank. They had two daughters, both in their early twenties, who had been well educated and were distressed that the war had interrupted their studying, one wanting to become a doctor, the other a dentist. Zejna the eldest could speak good English, and soon she was able to translate our story to the family. Amazed anyone would have come so far to try to help complete strangers, the family suggested the Aid should be taken direct to the hospital the next day but for now, some sleep was in order and we were shown into the girls' bedroom/study. The room was furnished with good quality modern, furniture and also contained a piano standing proudly upright.

'*Perhaps tomorrow one of them may play it for us,*' I thought, but for now the bed looked much more inviting.

CHAPTER 4

The Comforter

The next day we awoke to snow in Zenica, which had improved the grey scene in the market place. The inhabitants looked much like match stick men in a 'Lowry' painting, with drooping shoulders and bowed heads. Their postures conveyed the pain they had suffered when war invades overnight and catapults family life into a desolate hell on earth.

As arranged, Paul and I, accompanied by Zejna, made our way to the local hospital. She introduced us to the hospital director, Muhammad. He spoke no English, but this did not detract from his sincere welcome and the warm smile. Muhammad was a small-framed man with beautiful silver hair. He had just come off duty having personally delivered many babies the night before. He was proud to introduce us to various members of his staff. Their love and respect for this man was evident and straight away I was in awe of his gentle spirit and beauty. I knew from the very first moment we met that we would do all we could to support this man's commitment towards his patients. We would do it willingly and know we were privileged to be called to help.

He said the hospital normally catered for a thousand patients, but now, because of the war, there were about two thousand. They had no X-ray film and little in the way of painkillers. He particularly tried to impress on us the necessity of telling the outside world of their many urgent needs; although they had a normal supply of dressings, because of the nature and extent of the wounds of so many of his patients, there was now a desperate shortage.

Here was a deeply compassionate man who had already found a place deep in our hearts. We continued to be impressed by his care as he showed us around the hospital, personally explaining the patients' various needs. He told how, at the beginning of the war, that they had twenty working incubators for around two hundred babies. Now they were down to three.

The wards were crowded; beds packed in every available space. The midwife in charge of the baby unit told how there was no baby bottom cream and how they were desperate for teats for the bottles. Quietly I left Paul's side and moved cautiously towards the small cots. Although clean, most of them had two or three newborn babies packed into them. Each tiny mite was bundled tightly in an individual, closely wrapped blanket. I was thankful to know that each baby would feel secure being held so firmly. One baby was in full vocal flight whilst being changed, exercising his lungs to full capacity.

I moved towards him, his tiny arms and legs were blue and so very thin. Observing this child I realised that a simple thing such as a dummy, was something that we could bring which would give so much comfort to the babies, mothers and staff. Then I was drawn to a baby with an enlarged head. This child, though apparently peaceful, seemed near to death and I dared to ask.

"How long?" A doctor walking past overheard my question to the nurse.

"This baby will die because we do not have the valves to drain the water off the brain." I could sense his frustration. This was yet another situation, which illustrated the stupidity and inhumanity of war, and although I could do nothing at the time, the need for valves to drain the water off the brain was stored in my memory for use at a later date.

Some other babies quickly caught my attention. These little souls, so desperately ill were given individual cots. Some just screamed in fear as I bent down gently to comfort them. "Lord, be with these little mites. Heal their pain and cover their fear. Come in and dwell in them that they may know your peace, in Jesus' name."

Immediately a new presence seemed to flood the room, we all seemed to sense the God of the universe had come to respond to humble prayer, so both Paul and I continued to quietly move about trusting to bring a touch of warmth and comfort to each little soul. We must have prayed with over fifty babies, and all the time Muhamed smiled patiently, waiting, because he already knew any help from above for his little souls was the healing touch he welcomed.

Soon we moved towards the adult wards, where the smell of death and oppression seemed to hang like an invisible haze in the air. To see the grey faces and amputated bodies pained us deeply. Again my heart wanted to touch and pray with all of these broken bodies but I felt drawn to one lady in particular, who lay weeping. She could speak no English but with arms out stretched, "Help me! Help me!" she seemed to cry. She had a bullet wound in her arm, her leg and in the side of her stomach. She was also seven months pregnant.

"My baby, my baby, please help my baby!" She seemed to say. I reached out and clasped her out stretched hands.

'*Oh my God, what can we do? Please help!*' was my simple prayer. '*How can we help these people? They need your help*'. Inside I was angry at my inadequacy and at the same time felt drained and empty. The lady urgently pleaded with her eyes again, her arms reached out.

"Help me," she continued, drawing me closer, showing her wounds. Bending over her and trying to reassure her the best I could, again I beseeched the gates of heaven.

"Oh my God! What can we do to help? Show us! Please show us," still pounding the gates of heaven in desperate prayer. Bending down further, I took the lady's face between my shaking hands, and gently kissed her, inwardly promising to return with help thinking this must be a job for the big agencies.

Eventually I tried to extract myself from the desperate grasp but was drawn back into the morass of pain and despair. Soldiers lay with open wounds. The smell from stale blood in the sodden mattresses made my heart sink even further. Paul was touching my arm trying to draw me away. In a state of shock I must have pulled away and wandered from him along the damp corridors, mentally carrying all that I'd seen, taking deep breaths to try to restore my equilibrium.

Within a span of time for which I have no account, I looked into another ward where Paul was praying with an elderly man. My heart reached out in compassion with him, pleased at the beautiful scene in front of me. There was Paul at his most beautiful. This was the man I loved!

Apparently I was free to continue round the ward praying with the men injured in circumstances which I could not even comprehend. I tried humming a tune, trying to lift myself, trying to be cheerful where appropriate, joking where I could, but all the time my heart was being wrenched out and cut up. '*Lord, why do we do this to one another? Why? Why?*' As usual I had more questions than answers and still Muhamed the director stood near, love and compassion pouring out of him like some never ending stream.

Next, entering a ward of women, most of who appeared to be about sixty years of age, although they were probably only in their late forties, I approached a lady in a middle bed. She grabbed me with both hands; her urgency bordered on desperation and I was pleased Muhamed kept close. Already this lady was trying to tell her story. Apparently some extremists, most of whom in Bosnia are described as renegades, had come to her village on a night of massacre and destruction. Very much like Hitler with the Jews in 1940, they were programmed to cleanse the earth of all local population. This lady had been attacked and beaten unmercifully because she had tried to protect her granddaughter. Although I understood little of the detail of the story, I was drawn closer by the out stretched arms and the lady's insistence for prayer. Praying with her brought new feelings of total inadequacy. Apparently, this lady needed to go to the Sarajevo hospital for urgent surgery, but there was no way she could enter the city which was under siege. Her situation was desperate. The pain of her nightmare could be seen in her every gesture. "Lord!" I exclaimed once again. "Where are you? Come and meet with this lady. Put your arms around her. You know the way for her," I was pleading as I held her as tightly as I dared. "Lord! These people need your healing touch. Please don't respond to my lack of faith, but respond through your Holy Spirit. Let your Spirit come down and touch this lady in a miraculous way, Lord I ask a healing touch for this lady and for the memories of her family, again, I ask in Jesus' name. Amen."

Exhausted and drained I tried to pull gently away, but this lady had a tight grip on my arm. Unable to hold the bent position any longer because of the awkward twisting position over the bed, which was pulling my back, I moved a little nearer and hugged her gently again. I wanted only to love her better, her pain was my pain. Floods of words continued to pour from her and I wished I could understand more of what was being said. My concern was that the lady was putting her trust in me and not in God. Nevertheless, I kept silently praying in tongues until eventually she calmed again. Through Zejna I managed to communicate the message. "We will return to England and try to get all the help we can for your people." She seemed satisfied, so I was free to move on.

Next my attention was drawn to a little, round lady, sitting on the edge of the next bed. Her head was bowed, and she seemed to be trying to avoid eye contact. '*Lord, what is this?*' I was already inwardly asking as I moved quietly towards her. It was then I realised most of her face was blown away. Taking a big breath I just stood over her, placed my hands behind her head and gently pulled her into my breast, just like any mother would to an injured child. "Oh Lord, Lord, please come now and love her better in Jesus' name." I felt helpless and defeated and berated myself. "Why am I not better equipped to help more? Why couldn't I have been a doctor? Lord, what are we doing here?"

"Come on Jacqui!" words I could now only vaguely distinguish shook me out of my thoughts.

"The local T.V. cameras are here, we want to photograph all the gifts which you have brought."

"No! No! It's nothing! It's like we've brought nothing!"
Edo was standing by the van as they all started to unload boxes and boxes of toothpaste, soaps, shampoo, cotton wool mixed with bandages, boxes of beans, soup, meat and the occasional bar of chocolate which was viewed as something really special.

"So much, yet so very little." I felt sick, and I must have looked sick.

"Stop it Jacqui. You have done fine," pleaded Edo. "These gifts are incredible. You don't realise what they mean to us. Nobody had done this before you people." Both Paul and I smiled, grateful for what he was trying to do, but we were not convinced.

"We must get some real help for these people, they need more food and bandages, everything!" I wrestled with the flesh seeing only our limitations, yet deep down I knew God would move and He would honour our commitment.

More relaxed now we bade our farewells and made our way back through the darkness. Again we climbed the twelve flights of concrete stairs, again we reached the warmth of Nejra's sanctuary, glad to be back, to be able to get a sense of proportion and reflect on all we had seen.

"So this is Bosnia, Lord. These are the people you want to touch with your love. I can't see what little people like us can do in such a mammoth situation, but if you will continue to lead, we will continue to follow."

A little more at peace, we began to relax in the comfort of this home and much to Paul's delight, Nejra presented her home made dishes of traditional goodies. Sleep was not going to be a problem this night and it seemed no time at all before we woke to be greeted with a refreshing cup of tea the following morning. Our hosts were beginning to get the message about my weakness and addiction to the English habit.

My Mother always seemed to find the answer to life's problem by saying, "Let's have a cup of tea and a cigarette," and whilst I had no desire for a cigarette, tea had quickly become a necessity for me in this place. "Maybe there is a way of getting it intravenously?" Paul quirked. Now fully awake and dressed, I stood and looked out of the window.

"What's that big building over there?" I enquired of Zejna.

"It is a school housing 350 refugees. These people arrived, some walking; some in cattle wagons from when their village was over-ran. Many have been killed and these are the 'lucky' ones."

"Can we go and meet them?" Paul enquired, eagerly.

"It is not good for you two, especially you Jacqui." Zejna took one look at the expression of response on my face.

"Well if you must, you crazy woman!" she was by now treating me like her sister, and I liked that.

After breakfast we made our way down the dark stairs, across the road and into the school. As soon as we walked in the main doors, the smell of sewage hit hard. Undeterred, and pretending not to notice I followed on, I so wanted to get to know these people, share their pain and bring a little hope.

Having received permission from the 'committee' we made our way into the first of seventeen classrooms, all housing between fifteen and twenty-five people. At each door there was a collection of old shoes, most of which were only soles with bits of string to hold the old leather to the feet. We respectfully removed our shoes as we approached the individual families. They were living most of their days and nights on blankets. Each blanket marked out an individual territory. But could this be the school spoken about by the lady in England for whom I now carried the letter which was in my pocket? "Does anyone know of this man?" I held up the letter.

With the refugee grapevine working to the full, it didn't take long to locate Emir, the husband. He was hustled before us by a small group of bustling women.

"You Emir? Your wife in England, at this address?" I showed him the brown envelope, creased from being rolled up tightly. The man, who already looked ill, went a paler shade of grey as I opened my arms to him.

Receiving the letter in total disbelief, he dropped straight into my arms in floods of tears of relief. It seemed everybody was now crying. Man or woman it made no difference, this was a dream many of them had held on to as a means of keeping alive. We were all seeing someone's dream come true.

With joy, I kissed him on the side of his cheek, hugging him at the same time. "This is from your wife." The tears flowed faster. "Your wife in our home last week, very beautiful lady, very pretty." He tried to smile through his tears. Everyone was caught up in this emotional situation. Even the men cried, unashamed of showing their emotions. These people had lost so much, been through so much so they weren't interested in false pride. The more they cried the more we loved them, these were our kind of people, they were prepared to be open with their vulnerability, honest with their emotions.

It wasn't long before most of the women seemed a little brighter but the men were much more sullen, dull in spirit and countenance. One boy, who looked about twelve, was pulling at my coat trying to get us to go upstairs to meet his family. Paul nicknamed him Jimmy, as he had a look of Jimmy White the snooker player back home. As we followed Jimmy with about another twenty to thirty women and children trailing behind, we were beginning to feel like the Pied Piper, but what could we do for these people? We were impressed by Jimmy's unselfishness, asking for nothing except that his mother meets the English people. I searched my pockets.

"We must have some gift to give. If only we could tell them about our Saviour," I murmured quietly to Paul. But, for the moment, a piece of chocolate would have to be used to help build a bridge. Looking around the room there appeared to be only a few children, so I pulled out one bar of chocolate and cut it into as many small pieces as possible. Each piece was devoured in seconds and placed as the first plank on our bridge.

The grey faces were now smiling. They sensed warmth as the children beckoned for us to sit down amongst them. Zejna introduced us as, "These people from England," their smiles broadened.

'But Lord, I only have one more bar of chocolate. How can we turn this into 'the loaves and fishes for you?' I was concerned we had no more to give. One man in a corner was gesturing for a razor. Now, feeling a little more confidant, I gave him the thumbs up sign to let him know I understood.

"Paul, we have about 15 dinars in Bosnian money. Do you think we could go to the market and see what we could get? We must be able to buy some disinfectant for the toilets at least." He put his hands to his head as if to gesture, 'here we go again.' Having assured the people we would return and accompanied by Zejna, we made our way through the crowd and back down the stone steps into the fresh air.

The local market was only a few yards away, but most of the stalls were empty. Some had just a few second-hand items. I spotted a pair of old shoes, which looked first class compared to what we had just seen in the school.

"How much are they?" I enquired.

"The equivalent of £400," Paul worked out!

"Surely you have made a mistake! What sort of economy is this?" I asked Paul who was quick to grasp the situation.

"The cheapest thing we can buy for these people, Jacqui is money!"

He was right. Our money only bought a few rotten oranges and two pots of jam. But how was I going to get a razor?

At last I spied a yellow razor, on a little old table which was substituting as a market stall. I approached the middle-aged man with the usual Mediterranean craggy features "How much?"

"Don't be silly, Jacqui." Paul was saying; "You would need a fortune for that."

"Well in that case I will have a word upstairs! That man has asked for a razor, and he is going to get one!"

"Please sir, you give me for my friend, refugee?"

He laughed, "You woman, you crazy! Much money lady! You much money?"

"No, but I have a great God. If you will give me that razor He will send his very angels to protect you and look after you," I continued with great conviction.

"Lady, how I eat if I give you this?" With a broad smile, I replied.

"You can't afford not to! All I can tell you, God will bless you beyond measure if you give it to me." I smiled again. He looked and surrendered. With gratitude I thanked him, sure God would honour as I silently claimed his soul for all eternity.

Like an excited schoolgirl I looked forward to delivering one razor so we hurried back, eager to deliver the special gift. Zejna was speechless at what she had just witnessed and was happy to give it to the man in the corner.

We all intended to return to the flat but Paul had needed to go back downstairs to our van to change into some clean trousers for the evening. I was contentedly half way through my first cup of tea when there was an almighty explosion. The whole family instinctively ran to the hallway, this being the centre of the building and furthest from the windows. I ran straight to the back window to see if I could see Paul and at the same time to discover what had happened. Swirls of thick black smoke were rising up into the sky from about fifty yards away.

"Come away Jacqui!" Nejra was vigorously shouting. Zejna joined me on the balcony urging for me to leave the window area.

For a moment all was quiet. Just as we were taking a breath of relief, there was another *boom* from high over the mountain, a high pitched squeal, then… silence. For a couple of seconds, we all waited.

"Jacqui! Down!" Zejna shouted. In an instant I grabbed her shoulders by instinct and threw my own body on top of hers before we both hit the floor. An immediate explosion followed.

'*That's done it!*' was my first thought. Two more shells fell in quick succession and Nejra was going crazy, shouting for us to join her away from the window. To reassure her we surfaced quickly, but not before taking another quick check to see if the van and the school were still standing.

"Come away! Come away both of you!" Nejra pleaded.

"I must go and find Paul. I want to be with him," I found myself protesting. "It's OK Nejra, we will all be all right," I said firmly. Then I prayed a quick prayer, asking for a hedge to be put around them and the whole building.

As I reached the front steps, Paul was on his way back in and out of breath he was saying.

"That was close, I was just putting my trousers on when the first shell fell. I thought, Jacqui will go ballistic if I get killed with no trousers on!" He planted a quick peck on my flushed cheeks.

We were taking a moment to reassure each other when we were joined by a lady, also out of breath and shaking from head to toe.

"Man dead! On bike. Boom!" She was clearly in shock. We sat her down on the steps and huddled close to her in order to help keep her warm and secure. The lady put my hand on her heart area as I tried to re-assure her. "You ok"? No problem!" At least that's what my voice was saying, but in my heart I wasn't sure that it was the truth.

The lady indicated she wanted to go across to the school.

"That's fine. No problem! We'll take you!" Within a few minutes we were entering the school as most of the refugees were just emerging from the cellar. Apparently, in the cellar they use tables to form a catwalk to enable them to avoid walking in the sewage, which had escaped from the broken pipes.

The lady seemed to know which classroom she was heading for, so Paul and I just followed. When we entered the room we were shocked to find ourselves right in the middle of loud moaning and wailing. Over on the far bed a lady was prostrate, arms out stretched, her head rolling about. She had just heard her husband had been killed and was beside herself with grief. Many other distraught women were gathering round the bed, trying to console the best they could.

"Jacqui, Please! Please!" One of the refugees was asking me to go over to the bereaved lady. At first I was reluctant to intrude in her private grief, but now several women were urging me. Straight away I held her hand, then held her close to my whole body as my heart began to bleed alongside the widow's.

"Lord, please come and bring your healing balm for this dear sister. Comfort her and love her in Jesus' name." I looked deeply into the eyes of this woman. I could see and I knew her pain.

'*In everything under the sun there is a purpose*' kept going through my mind. What was the Holy Spirit trying to teach me? Hadn't I just prayed? '*Come Lord bring your healing balm, comfort her, love her in Jesus' name*'. Suddenly there was a realisation, He had, He did and we were it!

My mind flashed back to a day twenty years ago. Oh how I remember old Jack's words to me the day I collapsed into his arms all those years ago. He simply put his strong arms around me and said, "He knows, He cares." And he was right. The man, Jack Howells, knew all about suffering.

Jack had been a Welsh Rugby International in his younger days, who had been caught up in drink and, I imagine from listening to him, had his fair share of lady friends. He had been saved from his lifestyle during the time of the Welsh Revival and he frequently shared how one night he had run down the centre aisle of the local chapel, threw himself prostrate on the floor and begged God's forgiveness. From that time on he was a new person.

By the time I met him he was in his seventies; tall, lean and with a smile which reflected an intimate love with His Saviour. He had the longest arms I ever knew. He always said he only wanted to stretch out those long arms and put them round the hurting people and love them better. I was beginning to wish we could have Jack's arm's here with us now.

Oh yes, Jack knew pain. One day his twenty-two year old daughter was upstairs singing, "I surrender all... I surrender all," arms stretched heavenwards in complete abandonment. Within seconds she had fallen down the stairs and lay dead. Then as if from a broken heart, his wife also died and within a three-week period he had buried his wife and daughter.

Yes, Jack Howells knew pain. Yes, Jack Howells knew how to get alongside pain. At the very worst time in my life, Jack Howells had been love, in action, there for me. It had been Jack Howells who had handed over the baton in the relay race of life to me. It had been Jack Howells who had commissioned me to; 'Go into all the world and take the gospel message.' I was now without doubt that God again would honour His own word.

As soon as this lady calmed a little more, the other ladies seemed more willing to take over, so discreetly and quietly Paul and I moved away making our way back to complete, what we hoped would be the final scenes of this very emotional day.

CHAPTER 5

No Way Back

As we approached the school the following morning to say goodbye to our new friends, a light covering of snow once again improved the appearance of our surroundings. To our surprise a shivering Emir (the husband who had received the letter) was waiting, clutching one very small bag. The bag he was carrying should have given us some sort of clue as to his hopes, but the women who were gathered around, a volunteer support committee, distracted us. They began asking, pleading and then begging us to take him to another small town, in the hopes of maybe getting a passport. It didn't seem such a big deal but neither of us felt quite right about the request and hadn't yet learnt to say the hardest word: No.

"What do you think?" Paul asked, stroking his beard.

"Well I suppose so, it won't do any harm and who knows it may just help him get back to his wife one day." I realised that I had responded with unusual vagueness, so added, "but there's no point in us both having to suffer the red tape of form filling, if you would rather rest, I could take him."

Paul would have none of it and not anticipating any problem getting through the check points, we thought we were well on schedule to obtain Emir's passport and deliver him back to the school by lunch time. How naive we were!

The first office where we found ourselves waiting had dark brown peeling paint work. After about three-quarters of an hour we were told by a grubby looking man in an even grubbier uniform. "It is impossible to get a Bosnia passport in less than six weeks, and then only for V.I.P 's."

"What does that mean?" Paul enquired. "**V**ery **I**nflated **P**rice?" We had heard the going price for a passport on the black market was about fifteen hundred Marks. The thought of a thriving black market got well up our noses.

"We can't give up at the first hurdle and we're definitely not going to play their games. However, this man may not get another chance ever to see his wife and children again if we can't find a way through this maze of red tape. We'll just wait for someone with more authority to come." I was beginning to dig in.

The man behind the desk shuffled piles of papers with small photographs attached to them, but before I could formulate my thoughts another soldier came in through the door. Immediately, Emir shot to his feet to greet him.

"Dobar dan," the newcomer turned and addressed me courteously.

"Dobar dan," I displayed my only knowledge of the language proudly, hopeful of some points in my favour. Emir and the young soldier beckoned us to follow them outside as they were clearly discussing the situation.

The pavements were full of soldiers, each one carrying a gun and immediately I was having a job keeping pace with these burly men, whilst Paul strode on in front seeming to enjoy the male company. Trying to pick my way along the broken pavements, whilst at the same time weaving in and out of the heavily armed military, I was soon left meters behind. I wondered why God had not given me roller skates instead of feet.

It took about twenty minutes to arrive at another building and showing my lack of fitness, I was well out of breath after my unexpected hike. Again we ascended some stairs and now waited on the top landing, we sat on the old wooden chairs provided. The ceilings were extremely high and were all a dirty shade of cream. Once more a soldier shuffled papers back and forth as we all anxiously watched the time. It took another half an hour's wait before we were shown into the room behind the outer office.

The smell of damp filled the air. An old painting of Tito did nothing to enhance the room. I had the feeling it was only the paint, which was keeping the wall in place. The soldier behind the desk was unshaven, and where his hand used to be, an ugly stump protruded from his jacket sleeve. He barely glanced up as Emir stated his case and asked for a pass to be free to move out of Bosnia. As we watched their interaction, hopes of Paul and I getting out of central Bosnia that day were fading fast. After more wrangling and more waiting, we were eventually shown into an inner office.

"This is certainly the inner sanctuary, and that picture of Tito hanging on the wall, is a definite improvement on the last." Paul was trying to break the tension.

To my absolute amazement a smart, good-looking young man came and sat at the large desk in front of us. On hearing we were English, he immediately sent for refreshments before going over to a large glass cabinet. He removed a cassette and brought it over to the desk. In broken English, "Please, we wish you have this. We would have you know we still great people."

Graciously we thanked him. "On behalf of the English people, we would like to assure you, there are a lot of people in England who care deeply about the plight of your people. Many people in England are frustrated that our government seems unwilling to get involved further to help your people more."

"Yes we don't understand that, but thank you and your friends for what you are trying to do for my country-men, and Emir. He is most fortunate. I will be delighted to sign these papers, please do all you can to help our friend." Smiling and wishing us well, he signed the papers.

We could hardly believe our luck as we made our way back through the town, now quite comfortable walking amongst camouflaged, uniformed males until I spotted the sight of dozens of hand-made wooden headstones on the freshly dug graves. There was a profusion of photographs of dead loved ones displayed on every lamp post only a few yards away which made me feel quite sick and vulnerable.

I could feel the mothers' agonising pain in the loss of their young sons, and had to fight to break out of my own depressing thought patterns.

"As it is so late, it probably will be best if we take Emir back to the school now." I was already projecting my mind forward to the task of how we could possibly help him further. "If he has a passport and a visa to enter England by the time we come on our next trip, then maybe we'll be able to help him further." I didn't know what else to suggest and, thinking that was the end of the matter. "Let's go back and make an early start home tomorrow."

"Fine with me," agreed Paul, cold, tired and bored with the whole procedure.

We started on what we thought was to be a short trip back to Zenica. The journey went well even though by the time we were stopped at the first check point the snow had thickened considerably.

"Zenica?" I chirped to the guards, expecting no problem.

"No. Sorry Lady! Much fighting! You no go through."

"What do you mean no go through?" I questioned if my

powers of comprehension had seized up. "We have got to get through to take this man back?" At last coming to some positive conclusion. "Well Paul, it looks as if we are taking Emir with us whether we like it or not. We'll have to try and follow in the tracks made by the other lorries which are ahead of us."

"Actually we don't have any real choice," agreed Paul in a calm, matter of fact way, which made me want to hit him.

Over the next couple of hours the men frequently had to get out and push in the ever deepening snow, whilst behind the steering wheel I did my best to keep the van facing forward.

"I wish we could have gone back and started fresh tomorrow," I murmured as the cold began to bite into my bones. One didn't have to be an Einstein to see this journey out of central Bosnia was not going to be fun. "Let's stop at the first UN base and see if we can get the loan of some snow chains and maybe a hot meal."

Paul was relieved and pleased when we eventually arrived at Vitez, a small town where the Cheshire regiment from England did their best to help us. The burly sergeant after offering us a meal scratched his red hair whilst considering the possibility of snow chains. "Sorry, we don't have any chains which would normally fit this van, but we do have a set which are in stock by sheer mistake. It just so happens they don't fit any of our vehicles so we will cut them down and try to make them fit.

Just as all three of us were drooling over the thought of hot food and were about to walk towards the temporary eating-house, the Sergeant spoke again.

"Before you go, young lady," he said, looking down at my light footwear in total disbelief. "Lady, we in the army survive, to fight! You however, before this night is through, will have to fight to survive!"

It was a blow below the belt, but he was right. If we were going to come into a war zone, then we had better get equipped to do so. As we pondered in thought over a welcome cup of tea, we both learned a lot from the remark. We knew, we needed to become more professional in our approach if we were to survive the terrain and climate, let alone the fighting. We were grateful for his honesty.

"These chains should at least help you, maybe even stop you, from being frozen to death tonight." We thanked the sergeant warmly, knowing he had given us more than snow chains, tea and sympathy.

At that time the only road open ran through a Muslim/Serb front line. It was now dark and we tried to keep our spirits up by singing. Over the airwaves came a familiar sound "Oh when the Saints…come marching in…" Emir's face lit up, as he recognised the tune. Singing as quietly as we could we began to enter a pitch-black tunnel. Surprisingly, Paul accelerated. Puzzled at first by what appeared to be his reckless driving we realised he was trying to get through before the tune finished. Bonded together just a little more by Paul's kind gesture we travelled on deeper into the darkness.

Suddenly a flash of blue fire darted abruptly in a straight line across the nose of the van, jolting our senses. My instincts would have been to accelerate but Paul slowed down, waited, slowed down more, listened, then slowly came to a halt turning off the engine and all the lights. The snow glistened on the ground in the bright moonlight. We sat there motionless, like mice listening and waiting silently for the cat's next move.

Time seemed to pass in slow motion until Paul started up the engine, which catapulted us into instant vulnerability. Slowly he dared to drive on. The compacted snow crunched under the tyres. We had this overwhelming desire to be out of there but could only drive as fast as conditions would allow. I did not complain as he swerved in and out of fallen trees, presumably blown down by the wind. At least that was my explanation to myself. I didn't want to acknowledge any other possibility.

Deni's shocking remark "What they do is, leave an injured person in the road with explosives in their mouth," flashed into my mind. We were soon past the shadowy areas and the road conditions improved immensely as we approached lower ground without further incident. It was quite amazing when looking back over the landscape, how the trees actually sheltered the area once we moved further south. The fir trees protected the narrow tracks, the snow actually giving way to slush, then slush giving way to thick brown mud.

Paul stopped to check the route. "We need to take a narrow left turn over a ten mile mountain stretch," pointing at the map, but I hardly registered what he had said as my attention was caught by a group of soldiers standing by the road.

"Lift, you give lift?" One of the soldiers growled as he rolled about unsteadily, hardly able to stand. My concentration sharpened.

"Yes, but only one in the cab, the rest of you must go in the back." This suggestion offended them. They declined the offer, with the exception of one soldier who scrambled over me into the middle position in the cab, almost sitting on my lap. As he did so, I found myself withdrawing from the stench of alcohol. Emir used this opportunity to take the sleeping bag and curl up in the back of the van ignoring the whole situation as quite normal.

To be truthful, I found very little joy in having a smelly gorilla sitting next to me and inwardly thought '*Yes, I should have had more sense than agreeing to have a drunken primate in the cab in the first place. It's not a good idea.*'

Knowing we had been naive to accept the passenger, I tried to console myself.

'*If we get stuck in all this mud, then at least he will be another pair of hands to help push.*' Of course I should have known better than to tempt fate. We had only travelled a further 500 yards over the first part of the track when the van became embedded up to the axles in mud.

"Blato…Blato," our travelling companion was shouting.

"Mud! Mud! Glorious Mud!" except it was anything but glorious. It was thick, brown, slimy and, worst of all, it hid the real danger.

Paul could not see the huge hidden potholes and for our little van it was disastrous. The under carriage was so low to the ground that if we weren't careful, we would completely seize up and be held captive by this dreadful blato. Slowly and carefully we edged our way forward as our crude companion took another swig from his bottle, burping fumes of fire into my face.

Turning away I tried to cut off from him and concentrate on the job at hand. "Pull right Paul! Watch it! Be careful! Slow!" It was too late. The vehicle had hit a rock. A raw crunching, grating sound came from beneath the seats. We had grounded!

Paul threw the gears into reverse. The wheels spun, churning up a shower of brown mud upon everything behind. Now into second gear the van moved just a few centimetres but the back end was spinning.

"This won't work Paul! We are getting further stuck." He did not need to hear that. I turned to our new companion, now was the time to find out what he was made of.

"Come on, let's get out and push." He shook his head and shrugged his shoulders.

"Yes! You friend. If I can do it, so can you. Come on! Move your big butt over here!" His day as a passive passenger had ended.

He crawled out of the comfort of the warm van, and stood with an indignant expression on his wrinkled leather face as if to say. "Who are you to tell me?"

"It's simple pal," I went on, "if we don't move, neither do you!" Again I moved my eyes from his resentful glare to the job in hand. I knew only too well, I couldn't even begin to push that van, never mind have any real impact on it, and it was clear this particular passenger wasn't even going to attempt to help.

He just started picking his way slowly through the mud to the lorry behind, greeted the occupants, climbed into their cab and folded his arms in total defiance.

Paul was furious. "Look at that son of a bitch!" He moved to get him by the scruff of the neck.

"Slow down, Paul. Slow down. It makes no difference. We don't need him. He's the last person we need."

"You're right," he begrudgingly admitted, composing himself.

"Now, lover let me get in the driver's seat. Get Emir out of the back then he can help you push." I knew it was essential not to accelerate too much or too fiercely. Gently, Oh! So gently! We slowly inched our way along until at last the van gave a huge surge forward rather like a child being delivered from out of the womb. The mud gave up its hold.

Paul triumphantly gave a thumbs up sign to the lorry behind. At least...I think that's what he gave?

By now the moon had completely gone behind gathering clouds. "How much further?" I queried.

"I think this stretch is about sixteen kilometres then we should be back on tarmac." I said nothing but thought Paul was being a little optimistic. At that moment I couldn't even see us getting to the other end of this monster mountain without a few mighty miracles.

In the distance I could see the rear lights of a small, single-decker bus. It was higher off the ground than our van, travelling much faster, moving easily along and rocking merrily from side to side as it bounced along the rough road. Suddenly, it came to an abrupt halt.

'*Wow if they are stuck, we stand no chance. Please will you stick close Lord, I've a feeling it's going to be a long, cold night!*' I was happy to have my inner friend with which to chat.

By this time Paul was accelerating uphill, back end spinning. "Do you have to go quite so fast?"

"Hold on tight! I can't stop now!" Paul was right.

We bounced from side to side. I held on to the door handles trying to take the weight off my spine. Each time we hit back down to ground a fierce shock wave went through my whole body. It was as if my legs were being severed. The whole of the bottom half of my body was enveloped in a cocoon of pins and needles. "Paul, please take it easy. I can't take any more of this!"

"I can't do anything else. Just hang on." Hang on I did, until suddenly, with an almighty crunch, we came to an abrupt stop. We had completely grounded at the exact place where the bus had come to grief.

"That's done it!" Now Paul was concerned, and he had every reason to be. Not one of the four wheels was on the ground. We were completely incarcerated by the brown slime, held up only by the under carriage pivoting like one of those circus plates impaled on the end of a stick. Glad to be stationary for a while to enable the after-effects of turbulence to wear off, I tried to move out of the van but my legs were like lead.

"Come on, you stupid things, get moving! This is no time to pack up." With what little energy that was left, I willed my legs to move. "Lord, now what?" I was crawling out of the van door and into the thick, brown sludge. To my amazement I straightaway sank down about two feet. The mud was well up and over the top of my thighs.

"If it wasn't so dark, and we weren't in the middle of Bosnia, I might just laugh at this!"

"*Laugh anyway!*" Came the inner response.

From a distance we heard sounds of merriment and looked across to see some soldiers sitting on a mattress in front of a log bonfire rolling about, roaring with laughter at our predicament. "Come on, you guys come over here and push!" I mimed the gestures. This made them fall about laughing even more. Whilst I was willing to concede the whole situation must have been quite entertaining, I could not understand how they could just sit there, without moving a muscle to help.

"Come and help! You lazy…!" My blood boiled as I beckoned them.

By now the thick brown mud was over the vehicles door ledge. "There is no way this van is ever going to move without more help. Of one thing I am quite sure, we can't call out auto assistance here!"

I realised on such a narrow path, if any vehicle got stuck and blocked the way for others, eventually the drivers of the vehicles behind would just have to push the offending obstacle over the edge. There was nothing for it. I would have to put my pride in my pocket and try again with the soldiers and, maybe this time, just a little bit more sweetly. At least that is what a tactful woman would have done, but somehow I didn't feel sweetly disposed towards them.

Moving forward I was conscious of lowering the tone of my voice and could see they were still enjoying our predicament. "You guys! Just what do you think you're doing? Do you think we've come all this way for the benefit of our health?" I was now almost on top of them, gaining momentum. "Come on! Get off your backsides, you idle good for nothing so-and-so's!" Not the best way to get a positive response from the opposite sex. "Get this wagon out of here!" I sounded more like a sergeant major than a female from England who would stand no chance in becoming a diplomat.

They were so amazed any woman would dare speak to them in that tone, they just stood up and followed, half-bemused, maybe thinking I had some hidden authority, which they should know about. "Come on lads! You can do better than this!" I kept up the pressure, but softened my voice just a little.

It was obvious to everybody; all the pushing in the world was not going to move this van. It looked stuck for the duration. Under all the bravado my heart was beginning to sink, but I was determined not to let them see any feminine weakness.

In any group there is usually one person who will shine. On this occasion one of the younger soldiers, realising the need and taking full responsibility, started to take command. He gestured to everybody to wait whilst he waded towards an oncoming lorry. To our amazement, the lorry driver, at the request of this young soldier, produced a solid tow-bar. It took only minutes to get things organised and, very slowly, to the sound of metal crunching beneath our under carriage, all four wheels plopped back on to solid ground. Much to our relief we were being pulled towards the safety of the inside edge of the mountain pass, nestling into the bend.

After thanking them and feeling half embarrassed, not wishing to cause any more trouble, Paul and I decided to stay put in the curve of the bend and take a breather. A long line of wagons had gathered, some in front, some behind. Paul counted every one of them. There had been twenty-six held up on our behalf.

Conscious of the narrowness of the track I tried quite

unconsciously to contract my body, as if by getting smaller the van would also shrink. "Maybe, Paul, this would be a good time for us to become invisible."

"Maybe this would be a good time for Scotty from Star Trek to beam us up!" he responded back with his unmistakable dry wit.

Very slowly the train of vehicles began to move past. First one, then another, carefully and slowly moving past as I consciously tried to use my mind and body to edge us over to the inside of the track, but it didn't make any difference, the traffic was still only getting by us with only centimetres to spare.

"Oh! No! This one will never get through!" I gasped as a massive articulated lorry approached. We just sat waiting for the crunch. The huge vehicle came at us like a giant bulldozer. Paul, starting the van's engine, tried desperately to move nearer the edge. It was a futile effort. The thin screech of cutting metal set our teeth on edge.

"That's done it!" was my immediate response.

"Maybe it just sounds worse than it is," said Paul who was trying to comfort himself and at the same time wondering what the Van Hire Company in England would say. He jumped out.

"Oh! No! You should see this!" The damage was even worse than it sounded. Down the whole length of the hired van was one clean cut; the metal had been neatly sliced through like butter.

"How are we going to explain this in England?"

It wasn't long before the wind whipped up the glutinous mud, ready to ensnare its next victim. Clearly we would have to move on but this time we were going downhill and, of course, that made quite a lot of difference. I looked forward to a much easier descent until, sure enough, another white truck was embedded in the thick, brown slime, held captive by the treacherous, gooey stuff.

"This mountain track must claim more exhausts per kilometre

than any other stretch of track in the world!" There was only one thing for it, sit and wait and enjoy the star-lit sky until the white truck was towed free. I reached for my lipstick and as I applied it, took time to enjoy the constellations in the clear bright sky.

Paul moved forward, time for take-off! He revved the engine determined to plough his way through, leaving a good distance in order to give him the best chance of driving through the mud unhindered.

In the challenge of this anticipated mud bath we had completely forgotten about our passenger. Emir who was riveted to the seat, his huge, frightened eyes were staring out of his drawn, ashen face. Then, to our amazement we heard another engine roar into life. A huge JCB crawled from a siding and started to clear a way through all the mud ahead.

Like Cavalry to the rescue! Our way was now clear. I flashed a smile of appreciation at the driver.

"Thanks pal! Perfect timing!" Then looking heavenward.

"Thank you, Lord! You never fail!" As the speed increased I found the fact I could hold on to the side of the door handle quite useful, at least I could rise up out of my seat as I felt each bump hit the wheels. It almost became fun! It certainly wasn't what I would have chosen in my fifty-third year of life, but since we were in it. "Hi Ho! Silver!"

CHAPTER 6

Through the Darkness

We had only travelled about two kilometres of the sixteen needed and already it had taken about four hours. I anticipated we still had major obstacles to overcome, and it was nearly ten o'clock at night.

In these regions nobody is out after dark. These areas have to be defended daily and night-time is when the fighting starts again. Even the locals don't travel the mountains at night.

"Jacqui, maybe we should just decide to stay here the night. After all those soldiers back there were bedding down near their bonfire."

"Paul, I'm already bursting to go to the loo. No! Come on! We must press on. Why do you think all these drivers are so anxious to get off this road?"

Without words he continued to cautiously edge forward little by little. We managed about another four miles in the pitch-black night. The clouds kept covering the moonlight and the intermittent darkness only added to the tension. Deep shadows danced all around us and the ferry in Split seemed a million kilometres away. With the onset of the bleakness in front, I was beginning to think Paul might have been right to suggest we stay where we were. "Want a few sweets?" I asked passing them to the two men.

"Thanks lover!" Paul responded taking a few seconds to look over at me.

"We'll make it tonight somehow. Don't worry," he said, trying to make me feel better. I could have believed him, had it not been for the sudden loud crunch beneath us. That look and those words of comfort had cost us dearly.

"Not again Paul! I really can't take another mud exercise. What do you think I am… a hippopotamus?"

Paul tried to reverse his way out of the mud but we were only sinking in deeper.

"Paul, take it easy. What do you think you are doing?"

"Look, if you can do any better, come on. If not, shut up!"

His words went in like a knife. I knew I had blown it and also knew neither of us needed confrontation. "I had better remove myself or this could get nasty between us." I knew there was nothing left in me and I didn't want to make it worse as we were both tired. "Paul, I'm getting out. You'll do better on your own."

Letting self-pity and pride come into play I told myself, '*If he doesn't need me, then I'll simply keep out of the way.*' Jumping out of the cab, I found myself standing in the darkness, alone, up to my thighs in thick, brown, mud, I was not quite sure what I had done to be standing in this goo?

Convincing myself I would be more of a hindrance than help, I determined to keep out of the way until the four wheels were back on terra firma. With unstable ground moving beneath my feet and deep blackness surrounding me I stumbled towards a monster lorry in front. It was so high I couldn't even reach the first step up to the cab.

"Ok if I join you for this next section?" I shouted, out of my mind with fatigue. "You give me lift?"

The two middle-aged men smiled down at me. 'Locals?' Too

hurt and tired to care; I was now well away from the protection of my husband.

"You... Come up here!" one of the men seemed to say, putting out a grubby hand to help me. "You very beautiful lady. Where you go?"

"Split," I replied, wrestling with my internal confusion and adding, as if to re-assure myself, "My husband behind... in lorry behind."

The men laughed. Soon there was no lorry behind. We were travelling further into the darkness, bumping and bouncing. I began to panic inside as reality penetrated my thick skull and the shadows flickered through the side window. The branches from the overhanging trees were swiping the side of the cab as the vehicle gathered speed. The terrain was becoming easier but my heart was beating harder and harder. *'Where is Paul? Why isn't he here?'*

I felt like a child who had lost her father in the crowd. *'What am I doing here? Keep calm!'* I was saying to myself, not daring to look across at the faces of the men in the cab in case they thought I wished to be friendlier.

Taking advantage of the darkness, I allowed my right hand to feel for the door handle. Slowly and deliberately I moved my fingers over the cold metal and along on to the door panel. Nothing! *'It must be somewhere. Keep going Jacqui! There has to be a door handle'*

Still there was nothing and my heart raced even faster. I looked in the wing mirror; there were no vehicles behind us! *'Of course Paul is not there. He's way back, still stuck in that damned mud I expect'* I teetered between fear and hope whilst at the same time beginning to give myself a whipping for my own stupidity. *'Well,'* I reasoned, *'I put myself here – I must get myself out of this mess.'*

My thoughts turned again to jumping out. I felt again, this

time more desperately, for the door handle. The man nearest to me put his arm across my chest to indicate the door.

"Nema Problema! Nema Problema!"

'*No problem for you,*' I thought with little charity.

I decided to bide my time. The path ahead was still dark and, by this time, there were trees on both sides. We were travelling through a cutting in some woods. My heart raced. No other vehicle in front! No Paul behind! '*Oh! Lord! Forgive my foolhardiness,*' I called out of my heart like a child.

'*Who's to say anything dreadful is going to happen? These men may be perfectly OK. After all, they are just giving me a lift aren't they?*' The more I tried to reason with myself, the more I was not convinced. '*No, this is stupid,*' I decided, '*I am going to get myself out of this mess now!*'

Again, I felt for the door handle and this time found the place where it should be. The ends of my fingers moved over a small, exposed screw head. Nothing there! My heart was pounding like a base drum. Moving my hand further down the door I reached for the window winder... Yes! There was one! '*That'll do.*' At last my brain was back in gear but I would have to wait my chance.

Thank God! Ahead I could see some lighted cigarette ends moving in the dark, glowing like miniature torches. The lorry was slowing down! They were actually going to stop! Yes! It was a checkpoint. The barrier was down! '*S'trewth, I've no papers. No passport. No money. Nothing!*'

The driver leapt out, waving his arms, talking to the armed guard. The man in the cab turned to me as if to say. "You very pretty lady." I moved away as far as I could, putting up my hand to clutch the top of the zip on my ski suit. At that moment the driver at the barrier was calling my admirer to join him.

I breathed a sigh of relief. '*Now's my chance.*' Again looking in the wing mirror. '*Pitch black behind... only this small group in front of me! I must get out now!*' Searching for and finding the window handle I carefully wound it round and round until, slowly and stealthily, I could reach out of the open space. I felt for the cold, projecting metal in the dark. '*That's it! I've found the door handle on the outside.*'

The handle squeaked as I pushed it down: metal on metal. I waited tentatively... no they hadn't noticed the sound! Opening the door I jumped straight into the brown slime, jarring my spine. Not daring to look around I tried to move my legs towards the cover of the darkness. I couldn't believe the black density of the night. I could see nothing, absolutely nothing!

Frightened, like a child in the dark, I was consumed with aloneness and fear in the ebony night. Thankfully my legs were transporting me forward automatically, but I could hear the voices of the men behind me demanding I stop. "Hey, you! Stop! Polako (slow down.)"

I blocked the sound of their voices still needing to drag each leg about two feet out of the mud for each step. '*No turning back now! Just keep going! Paul is out there somewhere in this blackness.*' The thought of him pulled me along like a magnet, further into the darkness.

I reasoned. '*They'll not come after me in this mud. Good! They're not following! I am free! Free to go where?*' Nothing in front, except darker shadows in the pitch-black night as the mud squelched with each step I took.

This slimy enemy was well up over my knees as I battled forward. "I must have come about two miles in that lorry which means Paul must be two miles away... not even a torch! Why haven't I a torch? Everyone else in the world would have a simple torch!" I berated myself, punishing myself again and again for my own stupidity.

"Stop!" I could hear something in the distance. "Yes, it's an engine. Must get out of the way." I tried to move over to the left but sank down another few inches. The mud clutched at my boots determined to hold me in bondage.

Bright lights were now coming at me. I froze in the beam of headlights like a mesmerised rabbit. A soft 'peep' in the distance told me Paul had picked up my silhouette in the headlights. With a sense of relief and shame my knees began to buckle.

"Want a lift, Lady? Been having fun, dear?" Rightfully Paul was having his moment of triumph and rightfully, we would both reflect on my stupidity for a long time to come.

So far it had taken eight hours to do a sixteen kilometre stretch. Blato! Blato! I didn't want to see any more mud as long as I lived. There was as much mud on the inside of the van as there was on the outside, it was a wonder the wheels could still turn at all.

For one brief moment we seemed to be the only people alive. No cars, no lorries, no people, not even lights coming from the small shuttered houses. "We're not going to make Split tonight are we? Can we stop at the first house where we see a light and ask if we can park the van?" The 'little woman' in me pleaded.

"Yes, you're right, it feels awfully eerie around here. I wonder what our friend's feeling?" Paul was very graciously not maximising his superior position.

"There, Paul! Over there! It seems like a café type place." We pulled over on to the forecourt. Some soldiers could be seen inside the café, their guns propped up on the wall beside them.

"Paul, this will have to do. Let me go in first with the maps and see how the land lies." As soon as my feet touched the road, my legs turned to jelly. I stumbled into the café, trailing mud behind me, ashamed to be soiling the clean floor with dirty boots.

"Sorry! Sorry!" I was saying to the smiling face of the lady sitting at the second table. I pointed to my muddy boots.

"Nema problema! Nema problema!" responded the hostess. Relieved and putting the large map on the table I asked, "Can you show me where we are?" Realising the café owner could not understand my English; I pointed to the last place I could identify.

The lady understood and indicated a place on the map. Moving her finger a little further along she pointed again. "Where you go?" She seemed to say. I pointed towards the coast road on the map. The lady shook her head slowly.

"No tonight! You no get through… road closed." And she was without doubt right. There was nothing else for it, I went straight to my pocket and triumphantly produced a teabag.

Whilst my conversation was going on I took a sideways glance at the soldiers to check their reactions. They seemed to be quite happy with my presence.

Paul was now making his way into the café, having stayed outside with Emir to inspect the damage which ran the full length of the van.

"Jacqui you should come and see the van! What a mess!"

"No thanks dear, I think I can do without that pleasure tonight!" Tea was brought to the table and, delighted at the thought of hot food; we ordered some egg and chips. Again, the service was good and we felt quite at home and cared for by this lady.

She seemed to understand our predicament and, to our surprise and delight, offered further help. "Would you like to stay here tonight?" she communicated with hand gestures and a few words. She pointed upstairs. It was not difficult to get the message and we were most grateful to accept her gift of hospitality.

'*How wonderful, Lord!*' I was thinking as we followed her out of the café, up the stone steps outside and into her kitchen/dining room. It took only minutes for the lady to pull out a bed-settee from the back wall and carefully make up the bed with clean white sheets, whilst at the same time gesturing Emir to another room.

This loving care was a real treat after what we had been through and we took every precaution to avoid dropping any mud in her home. 'In as much as you have done it unto one of the least of these my brethren, you have done it unto me.' This lady had just brought this scripture to life for us, and we received the blessing. She would probably never realise what a precious gift she had given.

As soon as we snuggled under the warm bedclothes, I set about a concentrated time of prayer for her. Even though I was tired and had been on the road fifteen hours, the more I prayed the more excited I became. "Lord, please protect this home! You have said I can ask anything in Jesus' Name, so I am asking you, by the power of your Holy Spirit, to protect this home and family. Put a hedge around them, Lord. I ask it in the Name and in the authority of Jesus Christ." I knew the Holy Spirit was releasing His power.

All tiredness had left me and I was filled with so much energy I could hardly stay in bed. Thankfully, Paul had immediately fallen into one of his deep sleeps. I was free to praise and worship without disturbing him. I could hardly contain my enthusiasm. We had been on a physical mountain top that night and I was now on a spiritual mountain top.

As the dawn broke I peacefully put my head down for a quick nap before the household woke. It seemed only a short time before a little girl with fair curly hair peeped round the side of the door, and came to examine the strange lumps under the bedclothes. As soon as she saw Paul's bearded face looking at her, she hid again.

After getting dressed Paul fetched a two kilo bag of sweets from the van with which the child nearly made herself sick. "Come on, Paul! We need to be getting on our way, perhaps we have done enough damage with that huge mountain of sweets!"

I pondered on how we could possibly repay this lady for her kindness without offending her. Paul brought a couple of food boxes out of the van. The gift seemed insufficient and we were embarrassed. However, I knew we had already given her the greatest blessing possible, the covering of prayer. We trusted God would honour and keep this family safe throughout the war.

CHAPTER 7

The Milk Float

The following day it was only the fact we were heading for home which enabled us to keep up the pressure for another fifteen hours of driving before Paul finally, totally exhausted, stopped the vehicle. By this time it was 2.30am. We were at the top of another mountain road having completed the last uphill climb before our final descent down an ice-covered tarmac road which had not been treated with grit or salt.

The temperature outside the van must have been around minus fifteen degrees. Absolutely exhausted we tried to curl up in sleeping bags in the back of the van, but as soon as the engine stopped the temperature dropped and as we all became more stiff and cold, I just knew something radical had to be done. Paul was finished. There was no way he could drive another inch. Anyway, he was sleeping soundly and not wanting anything but rest.

Reluctantly, gritting my teeth, I forced my tired body into the driver's seat and turned the key. *'Lord you know I can only sit here. Will you guide this wagon back down to safety please?'* My eyes were hardly able to focus on the road, my spine and arms felt like one solid piece of bone but we had come this far, I simply had to help Paul as he was unable to help himself. We just could not give up.

We had planned to take the twelve minute ferry from a deserted peninsular, which would serve as a short cut in the long journey. The vehicle was skidding rather than being driven down the glistening narrow mountain roads and it's at these times one becomes aware there must be unseen angels supporting our frail bodies.

Finally, as we hit the coast road, the excessive cold gave way to torrential rain and gale force winds. As we approached Zadar, I knew the local militia were still pushing down from the North and I wanted to make sure we didn't make any wrong turns and end up in the middle of fighting.

Stopping on a dark, deserted, coastal road I spread the map over the dashboard. "Are we still on the right road? I think maybe we should be getting near to the turn off for the ferry," I shouted trying to wake the men.

Immediately, loud ferocious barks came from a nearby front garden. Paul and Emir leapt out of the back. "OK boy! OK boy!" They were trying to pacify the Alsatian dog when, out of the darkness and in the pouring rain, a small figure of a lady appeared. "Dobar dan. Dobar dan," she was saying.

"Dobar dan," we all respectfully shouted over the barking dog.

"Rex!" his owner commanded and pointed to the house. To our relief, Rex obeyed and disappeared inside. I approached the lady, holding a wet map which was disintegrating by the second.

"Ferry?" I pointed to the map, then to the way ahead. The lady raised her hand, palm upward to the sky indicating the wetness, then pointing to the house she beckoned us inside. We took no persuading to follow. The dog started up his loud barking again.

"OK Rex! It's OK!" Paul was saying.

"I wonder if the dog understands English?" I quipped in a small attempt at humour.

The home was large and well furnished. It had been a guesthouse before the war. One could imagine this lounge bustling with people, full of the bright lights, activity and the warmth of entertaining. Now one family was huddled together by candlelight in the cold.

Sitting with the father of the household was his tall son. This twenty-two year old son could speak good English, and it was not long before, over a meal, he was telling us how they were surviving. Although having problems feeding Rex, the family was determined to keep their pet guard-dog. They told how armed soldiers had confronted the father in a flat they owned in the town. The soldiers just burst in, pointing machine guns, and took everything of value away with them.

Just as the war began the family had been helped by one of their previous guests (a German) who had come to them with food supplies. He would have been trapped in the area had it not been for the son using his army pass card to get him on the last ferry out of the area. The family said they would be forever grateful for the courage and unselfishness of their German friend.

When they heard about our very amateur efforts they were emotionally moved and thanked us on behalf of all the people in Croatia and central Bosnia, Muslim or Croat. The son and I stayed locked in deep conversation. "You are my number four son." Two grown up sons of my own, Deni number three, now my seal was on this young man. I had inwardly made a personal commitment to him and his family.

After retiring to a spacious, bitterly cold but welcome bedroom for the night, Paul and I exchanged many ideas as to how we could best help the family and their neighbours. One thing we were sure about, there would be tins of dog food on board in future.

Having heard that the ferry was a sitting target, during the next two days we drove for another thirty-six gruelling hours to reach the Austrian border. When we arrived there Paul and Emir were asleep in the back of the van and I was quite nervous about what the officials would do if our paperwork was not acceptable. With very little energy or resistance left, I decided to play it by ear.

"Cigarettes, Lady? You have any cigarettes to declare?"

"No. I don't smoke," I responded, completely forgetting Meho had given me a packet of six hundred cigarettes for Ruza. "Oh, sorry I have these," I hastily admitted, pulling out a packet of two hundred.

The border guard snatched them from my hands gesticulating, "Ok You go." With a sigh of relief I drove slowly, automatically checking in our wing mirrors. By that time I had no idea what I was checking for, but merely acted out of instinct.

Finally, when Paul emerged and I had stopped at a service station, I asked him, "will you please go and see if there is anywhere, anywhere, I can have a few hours sleep?"

"No problem Jacqui! You can sleep in those empty cardboard boxes in the back of the van."

"BOXES! CARDBOARD BOXES! You are offering me CARDBOARD BOXES to sleep in after three days horrendous driving!" I was already hurting physically and now my emotions erupted with indignation. My pride was on fire like a beacon and Paul was about to take the full force of my hurt feelings.

"You two go and sleep in those cardboard boxes, if you think they are so comfortable and that is the right thing to do!"

To my amazement Paul simply took me at my word, picked up his things out of the cab, and got out of the firing line. Emir, not wishing to get caught in the crossfire joined him. Fuming, I withdrew to be alone with my own mounting anger. Every time I thought of Paul sleeping soundly in the back of the van, my frustration became stronger and stronger.

"How can he sleep when I can't even close my eyes?"

I turned the engine on, threw the gear lever into first, spun the wheels and with no thought for the poor souls still sleeping in the back; in fact especially designed for the poor souls sleeping in the back, I pulled straight out on to the motorway at top speed.

"Now, where? Which way?" I was asking myself through the tears of hurt and anger. Seas of headlights hurtled towards me; I went through long concrete tunnels; along stretches of endless tarmac. It was the energy from the anger that propelled me forwards.

After many long, dark miles dawn broke bringing some sense of newness. The sun began to penetrate my darkness. A beautiful new morning was being born.

Travelling became easier and I started to feel a little brighter by feeding off the rays of the sun. '*A nice cup of tea is what's needed now,*' I was beginning to love myself again but I wasn't so sure about loving my husband.

A log cabin type place which Paul and I knew well was coming up soon. "Great! We can have a cup of tea at last." I beamed inwardly. "Maybe the sugar in the tea will sweeten me up!" I was full of optimism and high expectation of the medicinal effects of the brew, but, when I pulled in I couldn't believe it… the cafe was closed!

Emir immediately took the opportunity of stretching his cramped legs and having a smoke. In total exhaustion I curled my body around the gear stick in the foetal position trying to rest and soak up more of the warmth of the sun's rays.

Paul stood back apprehensively, not sure if it was safe to approach me, the gap between us had become a chasm. The subsequent drive back through Germany, Belgium and into France did nothing to endear my husband to me, but thankfully we were nearly at the end of our journey.

It was 12.30 at night, Paul was driving and Emir as usual, was asleep in the back of the van, snuggled up in a sleeping bag. We were only about half a mile away from the ferry at Dunkirk.

"Oh, no!" exclaimed Paul, "I think we have missed the turn."

"No problem," I was forced to reply with an unusual amount of cheerfulness for the time of night. "Just go down this slip road under the motorway, and up the other side." For once, probably because of the strained atmosphere, Paul turned into the slip road stopping to check for other traffic before driving under the motorway bridge, but only in second gear.

"That's right! Go under this bridge. We're right. Go on! We can get up the other side," I urged.

As Paul moved the van steadily forward there was an almighty c-r-u-n-ch!

"What's that?" He shouted. I looked into the wing mirror. The road was littered with stepladders and dirty washing. Paul's muddy boots lay amongst some black plastic bags, in fact all our personal belongings were strewn over the road.

In one sickening moment I said quite pathetically. "We must have killed him, Paul! Emir must be dead!"

Paul shocked by my words naturally couldn't understand my comment.

"What are you talking about woman?" He shook his head slowly and tentatively climbed out of the cab. Looking in the wing mirror again, I saw him scratching his beard and looking up at the back of the van in disbelief.

"Oh! My God! What will the van hire company think about this one?"

I joined him standing on the dimly lit road to see exactly the full extent of the damage. The whole of the container part of the vehicle was hanging from, what we could now see, was a seven-foot high concrete bridge. It was a sharp, clean amputation. Instead of a Box Van, we were now pulling a flat bed truck! The only part that was still connected was the padlock to the roller shutter door, which lay stretched out as a carpet in the road.

To our amazement, still lying comfortably in his sleeping bag, but now looking up at the stars with glazed eyes, was our Bosnian friend.

"I think you would have been safer in Bosnia than with us!" I burst into uncontrollable laughter relieved that the tension of the last few days had at last been broken, even if in an unusual way. As I helped Emir to his feet to survey the chaos I could not stop laughing almost hysterically, which was infectious to the other two.

"Paul, I don't believe this is happening. It looks like one of those Keystone Cops films, where a lorry goes through a haystack and comes out the other side with just an engine and wheels."

Although we could see the seriousness of our situation Paul and I just could not stop laughing. "Paul, I really thought we had killed him when I saw all the washing in the road." I was trying to be serious through the tears of laughter, which would not stop flowing. "What are we going to do? Here we are with all this metal hanging from a bridge and the van hire companies name written in English, next to a port in France."

Holding my sides with uncontrollable laughter "Paul! It won't take much for the Gendarmes to figure this one out and," nearly curled up in two, "we don't need a tussle with French bureaucracy. Where's the number plate? Which half is it on?" Again I roared at the sight of what I was seeing.

"It's on the chassis half!" Paul responded, not quite knowing where my questions were leading us this time.

"In that case, unhitch that door and let's get out of here fast!" I was totally unaware that my laughter was boarding on hysterics, clearly from shock, so my decision making was not about to be the wisest I had ever made.

With no more delay we quickly gathered up the dirty washing, step ladders and Paul's boots and roped them all together on to our new flat bed truck! I climbed into the driver's seat, still giggling with shock but trying desperately to take control.

I could see the real implications of the situation and was by this time certainly questioning my own morality. "Come on, Paul, we need to get a move on! The consequences of this accident could be very expensive, and the sooner we are in home territory the better. If we are going to have a debate with authority I would rather it be on British soil, than from a French cell!"

Soon we were waiting in the embarkation compound at three o' clock in the morning, tucked in amongst the Long Wheel Based Lorries; our little flat bed truck was anything but inconspicuous.

"Paul, I keep listening expecting to hear the sirens of a police vehicle at any minute. Someone somewhere must surely investigate how half a British vehicle became suspended from a bridge in France!"

Our conversation was interrupted by a pointed question from the driver who was parked next to us.

"Where have you people been in that thing?" I struggled to keep my face straight.

"Well…would you believe?…BOSNIA!"

Note: We had the joy of seeing Emir reunited with his wife and two children in England after he was declared to the authorities and his passport held good. The couple went on to have another child and I called him, '*the baby that nearly wasn't.*'
Paul and I paid for the damage to the vehicle, which took a few years.

CHAPTER 8

Bluebell of Bosnia

Paul and I hadn't long returned from the last trip when Helen phoned to ask about our well being. Helen is an Australian; she is a big, beautiful blonde, one of those people who radiate life and have a heart which can reach through the skin of a rhinoceros. I met her when I was in business and we enjoyed a lot of fun together having worked on some very creative advertising campaigns. We have a deep, mutual, unspoken love and respect for each other.

It was not long before I was graphically describing the plight of the people of Bosnia and the heart-rending sights we had seen in the hospital. "Do you know, Helen, there was a lady who was seven months pregnant, with bullets in her leg, arm and stomach." It wasn't long before Helen's heart was moved into action. "Jacqui! Oh, Jacqui!" she was crying down the phone, "The poor soul! Just imagine!"

Helen had heard little, but had instantly put herself completely in this woman's place, and was experiencing the pain. "Oh, Jacqui, we must do something to help her. Jacqui, I can't handle this." Helen put the phone down, unable to continue the conversation. I was not altogether surprised and somehow I knew this particular lady in the hospital seemed to be the one whom God would use as a catalyst to focus our minds.

It wasn't long before the phone rang again. A much calmer Helen spoke with warmth in her voice. "Jacqui, Frank and I have decided we want to help this lady in particular. As you know things are, and have always been, tight for us financially, but we have two beautiful boys and in some way we want to say thank you to God." She went on, hardly taking a breath. "I have already made up a bag with everything for a mother and baby and we have put in a letter and a photograph of our family as we want to really show her there are ordinary people out there who do care and want to help."

Now, taking a deep breath, as if needing to stand stronger because she knew the cost of what she was about to say, "And we have decided, if she will let us know a bank account or something, we want to help her each month. We want to send her money to help support her in some way. She is now part of our family."

Tears welled in my eyes, and I had what felt like, electrical impulses running through my body. *'It looks as if Our Heavenly Father is at work again,'* I mused in silence. So it was to be. On the next trip in February we would trust to be back in central Bosnia just before the birth of the baby.

"Ordinary people, they're not just generous! They're just absolutely F-A-N-T-A-S-T-I-C!" Paul exclaimed having returned home after doing a food collection in a local supermarket. "I never cease to be amazed at the beautiful giving from the heart of ordinary people. Do you know it is real sacrificial giving?" He went on, "One lady came and gave a whole carrier bag of food, yet only had one or two items in her basket for herself. Another man came with twelve bags of flour." Paul was shaking his bowed head, in humble tribute to the caring generosity.

It wasn't long before the phone was constantly ringing with invitations to share in Churches and say a few words about our trips to Bosnia throughout the area where we lived. When Paul and I did share our experiences, I trust we did so in a simple and sensitive way, so much so that the whole congregation took the people of Bosnia into their hearts.

The love and warmth we experienced then and still do today, is part of the very foundation of what I believe is the purpose of God for the healing of a nation. To my mind it would seem that His love and forgiveness is His method of healing a nation. We have just been the hands and feet He chose to use. We hardly ever seemed to need to make any decisions for ourselves beyond surrender. The only thing, apart from our faith and prayer life, that seemed important was to be available and willing to follow God's leading like children.

It was only a few days later when the phone rang again. "Hello, my name is Mary-Anne, my husband and I are trusting God to sell our house to enable us to move out of the area but, if you would like, I will do my best to support your calling before we move. I know most of the local churches and members."

Within days wheels were spinning! Paul and I just stood back in amazement. I was no slouch myself, but when God motivates his people, watch out for the dust of the wheel spin! Invitations to speak came rolling in and the more we just simply shared how God was raising up his love for the war victims in Bosnia the more the love gifts came in support.

We could hardly believe it when, in a matter of three weeks, we had enough to buy a suitable lorry to carry all the food and wonderful gifts to His people in Bosnia. We spent days viewing all kinds of lorries and I was fast learning which types were suitable.

What we needed was an ex-army four wheel drive, but the more I looked at them the more ugly they appeared to me. "I just can't see myself sitting in one of those things – let alone driving one! Lord, I guess I'm not ready to be a lorry driver yet! Please give me a little more time to adjust."

The jump from working in a beautiful environment to navigating a lorry over rough mountain roads was a big one. I had no problem in being willing, but still needed to make the necessary mental adjustment before becoming a lorry driver's mate.

The very next lorry we saw was sitting comfortably in the corner of a big building, all warm and under cover. She was a lovely blue colour and had many extras.

"Would you like a test drive in this one?" the salesman invited.

"No. How much is it first?" I enquired with my usual direct no nonsense approach.

"£3,750, plus Tax"

"Big problem: we only have £3,000. Tell your boss we will give him £3,000."

"No chance! My boss won't accept that!" the salesman interjected.

I smiled again ignoring the whole discussion about money and cost. I turned to Paul, "I didn't even realise we needed a hydraulic ramp for getting the incubators on board. I didn't even know things like that existed, but God knew, I think He's brilliant! She must be ours!"

This time Paul made the offer. Quite sheepishly, "£3,000 is our offer."

The salesman laughed. "No chance!"

"Tell me," I persisted, "where is the owner of the garage? Can we speak with him?"

"Well if you will come back to the office we can phone him, but would you like to go on a test drive first?"

"No thank you." I already knew I loved this Blue Lady and also knew it would weaken our position to show any need of her.

On returning to the office I spoke with natural confidence to the owner on the phone.

"It's like this, we have £3,000, cash, and there's another lorry we saw this morning which we can buy. Frankly, we don't mind which one we have so would you consider selling this lorry for this price? We're going to have some lunch and we'll come back later for your decision." With that I firmly handed the phone back to the amazed salesman.

"Jacqui, have you gone potty?" Paul said in disbelief as we walked outside into the rain. "What are you doing? It's the best lorry we have seen in three days!"

"Yes I know and it's ours. But the owner just needs time to get used to the idea he's going to sell it for that price! Wait and see! Let's go and get some fish and chips, you must be starving?"

By three o'clock Paul and I were happily driving out of the yard in our new friend, Bluebell. She was an eleven-year-old, seven and a half-tonne, Ford Cargo, complete with power steering and full service history and what's more, as lorries go, according to a female's view of things, she was very pretty. I loved her already!

Imagine the scene. A suburban housing estate on a Saturday afternoon, but instead of families watching television or cleaning cars, it seems as if the whole estate was out in the street helping to load a seven and a half-tonne blue lorry, bound the following day for war-torn Bosnia. The families involved are just ordinary people, but they are achieving extraordinary things.

Hospital incubators are lined up, each in turn being packed to capacity, with packs of nappies and plastic pants. Large quantities of food, medicines and surgical equipment are being loaded. The wind is blowing a metal stretcher trolley down the road, much to the amusement of the gathered children. Hospital mattresses are everywhere and prove to be excellent packing for the valuable incubators.

There were boxes and boxes of supplies containing everything from razor blades to tinned food; heavy packs of hospital sheets and pillowcases all wrapped in heavy-duty sacking. Dolls and chocolates were being stuffed into any convenient space; it is as if they were saying, "We're going and we're equally important, so please make room for us!"

Large mugs of tea miraculously appear to warm the enthusiastic loaders. The high winds and driving rain work hard to dampen our spirits, but to no avail. Several hours later, as darkness falls, exhausted but joyful, neighbours hug and kiss, wishing well the ordinary drivers of a very extraordinary load. There are many heartfelt prayers for a safe return.

The lorry, the cargo and the high cost of sending such a gift into the war zone of Bosnia had all been collected and provided by hundreds of Sheffield and Barnsley people over the previous three weeks. Countless numbers of ordinary folk had been moved in their hearts to help support the call.

There, at the end of the day, stood a precious but seemingly ordinary wagon, full to capacity with thousands of love tokens. This gift was to travel 3,500 kilometres across Europe, through rough terrain and treacherous weather conditions, be exposed to grave dangers, and all to achieve its aim of witnessing to the love of God in action, and to fulfil His commandment to: "Love one another as I have loved you."

Jenny was a new acquaintance who was to travel with us on this trip. Although she would describe herself as elderly, like Bluebell she has an energy which would put a much younger person to shame. I would lovingly describe her as intellectual, mildly eccentric and a Socialist in much of her outlook. She has a deep commitment to peace and conservation, saving everything from the whale to the Amazon Rain Forest. Our shared desire was to do something for the plight of the people of Bosnia, but we had yet to work through our emerging differences. Personality wise, we made an interesting mixture but still needed to forge an effective working relationship. It is at times like these when I think our Heavenly Father has a wonderful sense of humour and must have been sitting upstairs smiling when we all chose to come together on such an expedition.

The fighting in central Bosnia was intense. There were daily reports of aid workers coming to grief. The UN had cleared routes over the dreaded mountains that they had named 'Triangle' and 'Diamond.' In fact, the morning we were due to leave, the news reported four Italians had been ambushed on the 'Diamond route.' Two aid workers had been shot in the back and killed, while two had escaped. I knew this would mean we would have to alter our route because the bridge before Jablanica had long since been blown up.

Because of the increased tension, Paul and I had learned to put to one side our personal feelings, willing to lay down our lives, for we knew that any holding on would make it impossible for us to go in the first place. Hours of surrendering our will, our thoughts; hours of checking our motives. It was at times like these that the prayers from our brothers and sisters in the Church would form the only basis on which we were able to travel. We were quite sure; it had only been their past prayer support which had lifted us above the enemy's grasp.

It wasn't long into the trip across Europe when I became conscious of the different value systems between Jenny and I. We each came from very different backgrounds, so it wasn't surprising, that small cracks soon started to appear in our relationship. Sadly for both of us, these cracks quickly became chasms.

Travelling through Belgium we had experienced a very uncomfortable time trying to restore our sleep patterns. Jenny had attempted to sleep across Bluebell's front seat whilst Paul and I tried sleeping on a single mattress on top of the aid in Bluebell's bowels.

Jenny had brought her personal belongings in a high-framed backpack and it was proving difficult to know where to fit something quite so rigid in amongst all the other items. As usual the aid was packed tightly and we could only just squeeze in our own personal belongings packed in black plastic bin liners. The simple task of retrieving articles from Jenny's backpack, ten foot up in the back of the lorry, was an immense challenge. Paul showed great patience each time Jenny needed something. After some time, I realised this exercise over a 3,500 kilometre journey would become too onerous. It was essential for Jenny to keep her overnight personal belongings tidily in the cab. We needed to make some changes, but I could see this wouldn't be easy for a woman who had a routine established over sixty-nine years.

I had a strict rule in the cab. "The floor must be kept clear at all times for quick and easy exit." This meant books, flasks and shoes needed to be kept tidy and off the floor. However, I had not yet managed to get Jenny to agree to this method of operation.

The only deviation to this order was the drying of our personal underwear or towels on the dashboard. More often than not my 'smalls' could be seen hanging from the indicator lever projecting from the steering column, usually much to Paul's amusement.

Without the growing niggles fully surfacing, we continued on through Germany and stopped at a service station for some breakfast. Jenny and I stood at the beautifully prepared display of fresh fruits, freshly baked croissants and trays of sizzling bacon.

"I'll have a bread roll and water. It's not necessary for us Brits to eat as much as we do!" murmured Jenny. Wondering if Jenny thought funds might be abused, I decided to modify my own intake and follow her lead.

Paul bounced into the service station, full of his usual joy and sheer excitement at the thought of food.

"Darling, take it easy," I urged quietly, out of Jenny's earshot. The words of warning

fell on deaf ears, so I tried again, approaching my warning from a different angle. "Paul, when your eyes see food, nothing else exists. You are like a nuclear warhead homing in on its target, with a heat-seeking device which would put NATO's defence programme to shame."

Jenny continued stating her disappointment about the way so many people over-eat whilst others are starving. Sheepishly I looked at Paul's plate piled high with food, and projected the guilt, which possibly Jenny wanted the whole world to share.

"Paul, do you have to be so greedy?"

Unconcerned, he looked me straight in the eyes and gave me one of those 'little boy lost looks,' which says, "Who me?" Now, for the third time, a clear open warning.

"Yes, you! Can't you hear what Jenny is saying?"

Paul was furious and came in for the kill. He hit back with full accuracy with me as the target. "I don't give a damn what Jenny is saying," venting his full annoyance and unwillingness to pick up false guilt. "Look, Jacqui, if you want me to drive that wagon, then I am going to eat what I like. I need my strength and I am going to make sure I've got it and I'll do and eat what I like!"

Reeling from this unexpected and uncharacteristic response from Paul, I allowed the light of the sunrays to feed me in a way the food in front of me could not. Jenny by this time was in full flight, lecturing us about the starving of the world and how she was proud to be still wearing the same shoes she bought from Oxfam, for fifty pence, five years earlier.

If Jenny had wanted to make us both feel guilty, she had succeeded with me but there was no way Paul was buying in to the tactics. I listened as Paul and Jenny each stood by their respective positions in the matter. Finally as we boarded the lorry for the long journey to the Austrian boarder I blurted out in desperation.

"You pair of hypocrites you are both acting as if you are totally innocent." Jenny huffed and puffed, shrugging her shoulders, as if what I had just said had nothing to do with her.

Neither Paul nor Jenny were taking any responsibility for what had happened. The more they did this, the more my feelings on the subject began to boil inside me. Over the long kilometres, I tried to understand the dynamics of the situation, yet I was sinking further into a pit of despair until finally I thought. *'Jenny can huff and puff all she likes, we are going to sort this out and Paul Ryalls had better start hearing or there's going to be trouble!'* Now it was fighting talk within my imagination!

The more I battled against my own frustrations, the more exhausted I became. *'Lord! Show me, what I need to learn here?'* was the cry from my heart as I sat in a sea of emptiness, detached from each one of them, feeling completely alone.

Paul could have been a million miles away. He was in his own world and as far as I could see, was planning on staying there. He was, in fact, mentally and emotionally, cut off from me. My adult self was asking. *'How come Paul can't ever see my need for his care?'* Then I remembered something I had read, which had been written by Ruth Graham (the wife of Billy Graham, the evangelist). 'Don't expect your husband to be a thought reader. He is not God. He cannot read your mind.' How often we women expect this from our men.

After hours of trying to reason, I moved my emotional self back into the cab. The atmosphere felt as hostile as before in the service station. Paul's eyes were firmly fixed on the road ahead which was the perfect method for staying safely away from us both. Jenny shrugged her shoulders up then down accompanied by big sighs, wordlessly showing her disapproval, as if fed up with the difficult child beside her.

It would seem neither of us knew how to get from the isolation in which we each found ourselves. As I saw it, both Paul and Jenny stood in opposing positions, but what I couldn't understand, was how I, the one trying to head Paul off from antagonising Jenny, still managed to get on the wrong side of both of them?

The fact was, I couldn't see a bridge, and didn't know how to build one and the truth was, I didn't know if I even wanted to try! *'Why should I venture into that bleak, unwelcome territory?'* I retreated safely inside my own thoughts. Maybe later I would lift up the bedclothes of my mind and peep out again into that inhospitable world inside the tin box of the cab.

Eventually we stopped at the Austrian border. The sun was still shining and we decided to buy some bread and cheese for the expected long wait at customs. There is one thing about the Austrians, they never disappoint with their bureaucracy. After driving several hundred kilometres Paul would need sustenance again before having to wrestle with the mountains of paperwork and ploughing through a maze of unknown foreign words.

If he came through this border unscathed and still smiling, you could take it his Guardian Angel must be standing on the very pages of the green, blue and yellow forms with which he would need to wrestle. "Maybe there is a special form making factory in this country where men sit locked in rooms, just thinking up difficulties for tired heavy goods drivers?" I quipped.

The whole exercise only took three hours! Paul was triumphant. However his joy was short lived, as we were only fifty meters from the next border where the whole process had to be repeated. We were again in another endless line of giant, crawling, snail-like lorries.

As we continued our quest to the other side of the border the sun was beginning to beat down. No sharing of food or drink could, by this time, bridge the gap that had developed between the other two and me. I just had to sit with my discomfort and work it through. I concentrated on navigating as efficiently as I could, trying to justify my existence.

We were four hours out of Austria and into Slovenia and I had hardly noticed the beauty of the scenery, only occasionally emerging from under my thick dark, cloud for a quick glimpse at the outside world. '*Why does Paul do this? Why does he leave me in this? Why doesn't he help?*'

As the kilometres were eaten up, we made our last stop before the Croatian border. Now something would have to break. There was no way we could even attempt to get through that border without being right with each other. I decided to confront them both. "We need to sort things out. We need to talk things over." The other two were not interested in discussion. They were more interested in refreshments, so again went to the services to eat.

By this time Paul could do no right in my eyes. The food was terrible and as far as I was concerned the whole stop was a complete waste of time. I definitely would not go forward into Croatia with this negative atmosphere between us. Neither Paul nor Jenny wanted to spend time clearing the air, and I was by now convinced that both of them were playing the game of justifying their own positions at my expense.

I felt I was being ostracised by both of them, yet the starting point was when I tried to get alongside Jenny in her bread and water exercise. Then I tried to warn Paul trying to protect him from being judged as over indulgent. Yet I reasoned, was Paul over indulgent? No, certainly not. Of course he needed to eat properly, certainly they both stood in opposite ends of the need to eat spectrum. Maybe I could have said to Jenny "Bread and water may be OK for you, but Paul needs to keep his strength up if he is to drive this lorry".

In addition I found myself not willing to play the game of perfect people, knowing this would mean accepting a false peace. Instead I decided to confront the rubbish and decided to invite the other two to do the same.

After much painful discussion, the door of understanding finally opened, enabling us all to build a bridge and share responsibility for keeping the channels of communication free, honest and positive. This helped us all to reach a deeper level of respect and love for one another, which was exactly what we would need if we were to survive this pioneering mission.

Somehow, a third person seemed to upset the balance of teamwork which Paul and I had established. Nevertheless, we were all acutely aware the very friction was of value. We were being finely honed, more finely tuned, and we can all honestly look back on our experience and say it was not easy. For all of us 'Grace' would need to become the cornerstone of our relationship. We knew we had a deep love for one another, not because it just happened, like falling in love, but because we all made a conscious decision to accept our differences, and love one another as the 'Big Book' says. We all found victory in forgiveness, something none of us could live without.

During the next few days we were to see why God had allowed us to fight so hard to come into harmony with each other in obedience to His call. Coming through that painful situation was only going to be a forerunner of what was to come.

"Just look at that! Talk about Bosnia burning." We could see, in the distance, a pale green haze in the sky. "I suppose it's a cloud of sulphur created by consistent bombing." The heart of ex-Yugoslavia was truly burning. Fearfully we travelled into the unknown, against all advice, to reach our goal: Zenica Hospital.

We were expecting a three day drive through bandit country where stories of ambushes of aid lorries were shared daily amongst army personnel, but for us all, at 10.30 at night, we were to experience our first battle against Croatian bureaucracy.

We had already been on the road for twelve emotionally painful hours. Slowly we pulled into the parking space alongside the customs offices, showing our passports at the barrier.

"Spedition!" The guard ordered us over to the offices. Fortunately we knew the routine. This was the time for patience, endurance and, if possible, big smiles.

The Croats were at all-out war in central Bosnia, so there was no reason on earth why they should allow us through to feed people whom they saw as 'the enemy.' We were totally relying on God to open this particular door for us. The officials took one look at our 'T' form stating that our destination was Zenica Hospital.

"No Zenica. You go Zagreb!"

"No Zagreb. Yes Zenica Hospital," I contradicted. Yes, they would let us go and deliver our aid into Croatia's capital city but not to the perceived enemy. This performance went on for over an hour. I even produced a letter bearing a Croatian stamp, which stated we were to deliver incubators to the hospital for Croatian babies. No joy, they simply weren't interested.

"You stay! No go. You pay 80% your load value, to go through."

'*80%! You really are joking!*' I thought for a moment.

"Can you tell me how much 80% of our load is?" I was indignant at the mere thought of it. "We are going to Zenica Hospital." was my repeated affirmation! "You can decide what you have to do to make it OK for you to let us through but, trust me, we are not paying any 'per cent.'"

The official in charge became more and more frustrated and agitated with the English woman. He marched up and down outside the office to recover his composure.

At that moment a busload of seemingly well inebriated travellers were returning from some sort of celebration. We looked on in amusement as the men behaved just like children who had been let out of school to play. Watching them 'perform' on their ridiculous rubber legs provided us with light relief from our own situation. Eventually, the bus was let through, and the guards returned to the English problem which simply would not go away!

After another hour of negotiation the officials finally gave in but only after I bent over their shoulders to see the computer screen and realised they were playing a computer game. I was furious.

The truth was, by then they wanted to finish their game and the English woman looking over their shoulders was spoiling their concentration, not to mention causing embarrassment. We were now free to press on into the war zone.

CHAPTER 9

Decision Time

We were trying to find the address in Zagreb, Croatia, where Deni lived with his mother since they had been evacuated from Sarajevo a few months before. We had seen the rather tasty sandwiches his mother had prepared for Deni on our second trip and I had a mental picture of an elderly, homely, mother-type person, so was quite taken aback when introduced to Ruza. She looked about the same age as me, well spoken but seemed quite wary. Still, underneath her reticence I discerned she was my type of 'woman's woman,' if there is such a person.

We all knew we would soon come to love her but there was little reason for her to trust us. After all she spent most of her days and nights with a radio clasped to her ear, listening to front line reports of killings and atrocities. She lived with almost permanent anguish in her mind. Was it surprising she was smoking about sixty cigarettes a day?

Not long after our arrival, Ruza had calmly gone into the kitchen and prepared a meal, having first brought a tray of Caj made from one of our English tea bags, which I now always carried with me. Paul tells me I am a Philistine where tea is concerned, but for me a cup of tea always restores my sense of home comfort. I mimed my joy of tea to Ruza in an attempt at small talk, without any understanding of each other's language.

Soon Deni and his mother began to tell of their fears about the war, how at any time, they could expect the military to burst in and maybe try to kill them. Deni said he would have no hesitation in killing his mother to prevent her being taken by the enemy. Naturally we were all shocked by this. I was not sure who 'the enemy' was and didn't want to get involved in the politics, but I was taking in the situation. I thought, *'There's Ruza she's lost both her homes, has one son in America and her other son Deni, is now trying to get his mother to allow him to join the Bosnian army. Her husband Meho, who we had met in Split, was back in central Bosnia, and she has not seen him for over a year. Gosh! It's not surprising she looks drawn and without much joy.'*

I was beginning to appreciate the depth of the intense pain within Ruza and the darkness which had all but overwhelmed her. I instinctively wanted to reach out, put my arms around her and somehow make her better, but sensed without doubt I didn't yet have permission.

With the help of Deni interpreting I asked very tentatively. "Tell me Ruza, have you ever thought about prayer?"

"What's the point? God no listen!"

"Ruza, how can you say that? Did you pray for help before you met us?" She had to admit sheepishly that she had.

"Then tell me," I went on, directing my next question to set up a final move. "What do you think we are doing in your lounge now? Please don't tell me 'God no listen.'" Ruza smiled a smile that simply said, "Checkmate".

Silently I prayed, *'Lord, will you please, please allow us to be a channel of your healing love to this very beautiful lady, tenderly heal the hurts. Keep her and her family safe and, most of all, let her know your love for her.'* Without thinking, and as if on automatic pilot, I reached for my lipstick, unconsciously offering it to Ruza just as a man would offer a swig of whisky to a mate. This gracious lady appreciated the sentiment and just as unconsciously, smiled and accepted the gesture without a second thought. The gap had been closed. Unexpectedly and irrevocably bonded together forever.

Ruza and I sat for many hours, following every news report on television about the local fighting situation. Village after village was falling, first to the Croats then to the Muslims.

Paul and I were to learn checkpoints along the way into central Bosnia could change within hours, so selecting the right documents and routes would become a work of art. I was beginning to get the message; creative paperwork was the order of the day! I knew I needed to collect rubber stamps on paper, like children collect train numbers. The more official looking stamps I could compile on the original paperwork the better, and the more chance there would be of getting through, but for sure we would not succumb to the pressure of giving bribes.

As we continued to listen to the news reports, we heard there was heavy fighting around Zadar. The Serbs were shelling the whole area. The news broke that a vital reservoir had been blown up and the Croats were desperate. British engineers were being sent to the area immediately, to give technical advice. We felt quite proud to be British and had never before quite realised the privileges and advantages of a British passport.

To learn as much as possible I sat night and day, in a dense blue smoke-filled room, listening to every news report (most of which I could not understand) trying to piece together the political situation. It transpired Ruza was a Croat and Meho a Muslim, each of course with different passports. Deni had two passports, one of each, and used which ever was necessary for movement between his mother and father.

Ruza told us how, in the earlier part of the war, she helped

Meho out of Sarajevo and up country, using her Croat passport through checkpoints. Now things were much worse. There was hardly any civilian movement, and thousands and thousands of families were split apart, anxious for news of loved ones.

The more I began to understand the situation the more I asked myself. '*How responsible am I for Paul and Jenny? I need to hear your voice. Which route should we take? And most of all when?*'

After several days we felt the time was right to leave. Ruza asked us to call on her brother who lives just on the border between Croatia and central Bosnia. When we eventually met him we discovered he was a Professor, teaching sixteen to eighteen year olds. This beautiful man, reflecting gentleness and kindness, clearly found conflict between the way the local political system worked and his own inner sense of right and wrong. He found himself quite unpopular at college by refusing to take bribes to give good marks to unworthy students. His fellow professors no doubt felt he was not one of them.

Paul and I could really understand the strain on such a man who was walking such a narrow tightrope between loyalty to his entire party upbringing, and the need to live by his own conscience.

We were to learn this beautiful man was willing to endanger not only his own life, but the lives of the rest of his family, by supporting his two nephews who were in hiding under his roof. They had escaped the brutalities of an invasion of Mostar, in southern Bosnia. The oldest nephew was twenty-nine and could speak excellent English. His brother, twenty-six, did not or was not willing to communicate so openly and kept himself separated in another room with the two teenage children of the household.

Six of them lived in a one-bedroom basement flat, which was a model of neatness and cleanliness. The family's resources seemed to bear up well under the constant extra strain of feeding these two extra, hefty young men.

The young men's father was a Serb and had been a top official before the war. He was like the captain of a ship, determined to remain on deck until the last part of his ship sank into oblivion. Their mother is Ruza's sister and a Croat.

Somehow this lovely family had survived intact despite the difficult political situation, constant bombing and internal exterminations. However, one only had to look into the eldest young man's eyes to see the deep, ingrained fear etched there. One day he was like any other young man training as an engineer, courting a young lady, when overnight he, like the rest of the community, was plunged into a nightmare of sinister violence and hatred, which drew ordinary families into a life of terror and fear. The strain of the present situation was certainly taking its toll.

Paul, Jenny and I with the residents of the house sat around the small white kitchen table as the eldest nephew tried to share his experience of life in the situation.

"You people must turn back," he was saying. "This is no place for you. These people are crazy. You don't understand. They are sick in their minds!"

The more I listened the more I heard his deep entrenched sense of hopelessness and fear. He saw no future for his country or his family. They were trapped. Not wanting to fight or kill yet, in holding this viewpoint they were held as traitors by their own school friends and neighbours.

The more I tried to explain why we were trying to help his country, the more insistent he became that we should walk away and go back to England while we could. "You people don't understand, you don't stand a chance of getting through. They will just cut you down!" Lowering his eyes he added, "Or even worse.

Why? Why?" He queried. "This is not your war. You don't have to be here?"

Gently I looked deeply into his eyes and smiled, "Please, can you just accept God has planted a seed of love deep into our hearts for you people. We come simply in obedience, as a direct result from how He has saved us from ourselves. Your people are not forgotten!" He gestured with his hands in the air unable to compete with this crazy woman! There was little political or spiritual understanding between us but we knew we were to be one family.

Paul continued to ask various questions about the fighting factions. He needed a greater understanding of the political situation. I went deeply into my own thoughts wondering how we could help. "Tell me young man, have you ever thought of leaving this country completely?"

Roars of laughter at my naivety. "Have we ever thought of leaving? You have to be joking it's the only thing we people ever think about!"

"Then maybe we can encourage you in some small way?"

He stretched his hand out to my arm. "Please, maybe one day, but how can we leave? Our parents are still in Mostar."

Even more gently now, I dared to reply, "You know, if I were in your mother's shoes, the deepest desire of my heart would be for my boys to be safe, that's what would give me the most comfort."

He fixed his gaze on me again, "I tell you, at this moment, we are still one step up from the bottom. When we get to the bottom line, then, well, maybe." I knew for him, he was right and I understood what he was saying.

"OK friend. But please don't leave it too late." Again he looked away with a deep sadness within.

"Maybe one day?"

I was beginning to feel the weight of our own situation. Should we go forward and try to get to the hospital and the refugees at Zenica against all the odds, or should we return home? I knew I would make the final decision, taking into consideration Paul and Jenny's lives were at stake as well as my own.

The family was quick to respond and like every single home we had ever visited in Croatia or Bosnia-Herzegovina, the families gave their guests their best accommodation and continued to plead with us to turn back. "Tomorrow, we will have a day of listening to what God is saying to our hearts," I announced, "Then we will make the final decision; but for now folks, does anyone mind if we try to just sleep?"

Paul had no problem eating and sleeping under the most difficult of circumstances, but for me that night, peace within seemed as unattainable as peace for that country.

The following day I decided to see what guidance God would give us. Would it be safe for us to go forward? Would we get through? We decided it would make sense first to travel to the pilgrimage town of Medjugorje in the hope of receiving some direction.

So within no time at all, Paul was driving Bluebell up the main street and we soon heard the sound of sweet singing accompanied by a solitary guitarist playing under the shade of a big tree. The nearer we moved towards the familiar sounds, the more we recognised our own church choruses. The musical group was made up of six Germans and, although they were singing in their native tongue, it was easy for Paul, Jenny and I to join in humming the well-known tunes. Within about twenty minutes we were all taking turns at choosing our favourite choruses and singing in deep worship.

In the midst of this sharing I spotted an elderly lady sitting weeping nearby. As quietly and unobtrusively as possible I approached, sat down silently next to her and took her frail hand gently in mine. We could speak no words in each other's language but that was no barrier to the moving of the Holy Spirit.

Although I sometimes questioned the value of my own feeble prayers, I trusted and started to pray silently in tongues knowing my Heavenly Father understood and would listen to the needs of the elderly lady. Face heavenwards, I looked forward to the day when all would be revealed.

As I moved back into the group the lead instrumentalist approached us.

"God has just laid it on my heart to pray for you and your friends, constantly over the next week."
I took a deep breath and smiled. "Thank you! Please do just that. It is necessary, in fact, absolutely vital! We all thank you most sincerely."

Having received the encouragement for which we came, we decided to go next to the Croatian/Bosnia border and test the paperwork. In theory there was no way we should be allowed to pass through, so the outcome would be a good guideline as to God's further will in the matter.

We approached the border with much trepidation, partly wanting to be turned away, but the other half willing to follow in faith.

With a deep frown the main guard examined our quite flimsy papers. Then looking me directly in the eye, he gave a broad smile, "Good luck lady," and beckoned Bluebell to go forward! Taking deep breaths and fixing our eyes forward we preceded into the unknown.

We were now heading towards East Mostar which would be

Muslim territory and I suggested we take the next left turn over a main river bridge. Bluebell went happily forward and we were all feeling a little more relaxed as we climbed the incline onto the bridge. "Paul, wait! This bridge isn't going anywhere!" True enough we were just heading into actual deep water. The bridge had already been blown up. It was in three sections. From our angle an optical illusion made it appear normal, but in fact it was broken in two places.

Paul reversed Bluebell, swinging her round as we headed forward again. Sensing many eyes watching, Paul took no persuading to jam his foot down hard on the accelerator!

"OK, let's try just one more thing before we go forward. Let's back track to the UN base," I suggested. "If anyone is going to tell us to go home it will be them. They hate 'amateurs' and will be only too willing to discourage us."

Struggling with an ordinary road map, I hoped it could guide us over the difficult network of narrow mountain roads. It took some hard driving to find the UN base but eventually we pulled into a large compound with a factory-type warehouse. We were still testing and searching for confirmation that we were following God's route in His time.

The place was deserted and there was a strange atmosphere. Food was piled to the ceiling; all boxed and marked with the familiar blue starred label.

"Anyone home?" I called out, but the only answer was the echo of my own voice.

Eventually a middle aged man appeared.

"Can you help me? We are trying to get some incubators through to the hospital in Zenica."

"Umm!" He bowed his head. "Things are bad. The men have all gone to a funeral. One of our wagons was blown up yesterday.

The Croatian guide was killed and the driver badly injured. The trouble is," he went on, "there happened to be an Italian T.V. crew following and they sent the pictures back via satellite and the victim's pregnant wife saw them in Denmark on her television screen. So as you can see, things are not good. They are all at the funeral. What is it you need?"

"Well I think one of your UN rubber stamps on our customs papers would help."

"Sorry, I can't help with that," he replied, "Go and see if the officers will help."

I thanked him and returned to the cab. "Paul, park right outside the offices at the far end please, wait there if you will and let me see what the situation is."

'Lord, please show me clearly, I don't want to make any mistakes. Paul and Jenny's lives are at stake, so please make the way and your will for us clear.'

A self-assured young lady approached me. "Can I see one of the officers please? We are English and are trying to get to Zenica," I explained.

"No chance," was the confident reply? "Our lorries haven't got through for seven weeks."

Totally unmoved by this comment I stood my ground as the young lady picked up the telephone and spoke into it. Within minutes a tall, blonde good-looking Swedish officer appeared around the door.

Even my faithful eyes could not help but notice his immediate charm. I responded naturally, trying to bridle my femininity.

"We are heading to Zenica hospital with incubators on board, we have done it before so may I ask what is the present situation?"

"Well," he stroked his chin thoughtfully, "if you have survived at this stage of the war, then I count you professional enough to know what you are about. Where's your lorry?" he asked, looking out of the window and stroking his chin again. I indicated Bluebell.

"That blue one down there!" he exclaimed in utter disbelief. "No chance! You will never get that over that terrain. The only way forward is over the 'Diamond' route and there's heavy fighting through Gornji Vakuf. Lots of sniper fire."

"Yes, we've been that way before and, you may think this a bit strange, but this is God's work, so we will rely on Him opening the way forward."

"You have done this trip before? In that? Well, given you are still alive and still willing to go, you might just pull it off, but not in that lorry." He seemed to think again. "If you are determined and you are quite sure." Then as an after thought. "You wouldn't like to take some wheelchairs for us… would you?"

To my amazement he continued planning. "I suggest you call at all the UN camps en route, then they will know of your whereabouts and will be able to tell T.S.G. your position. Please ask for a Major Bowers at Tomislavgrad. Tell him I sent you and I am sure you will get all the help you need."

"Thank you, thank you very much indeed." I felt totally released inside, if he thought we could do it, then we could do it.

With confirmation, and my confidence back on line, I dared to ask. "Incidentally, have you one of those UN maps? I could do with a decent map!" He gave me a broad smile and left the room, returning shortly with an official UN route map, which even showed the up-to-the-minute front line positions. We shook hands warmly.

The young lady stood up amused by the outcome. "Come on I'll get the necessary paperwork done for the wheelchairs and we'll get them loaded. You do have room don't you?"

"Of course!" I chirruped, secretly hoping we had, realising we had been given a great deal more than wheelchairs. Not only did we have official UN paperwork, but at last we had been acknowledged, and the UN knew we were on the map! '*Thank you Lord! You don't miss a thing do you!*'

Before long we were loaded and on our way. The pieces were in position on the chessboard. There were no more questions to be asked 'upstairs.' I turned to Paul and Jenny, "We will go back to the uncle's house and make an early start in the morning if that's OK with you both?"

CHAPTER 10

The Parting of the Red Sea

The next morning was bright and sunny when we set off taking the eastern route, north into Bosnia, enjoying the drive to the first UN base about two hours away. We thought we could find it without too much trouble by using our new map. This was new territory for us and Paul was quite impressed with my navigational skills. I had to admit, I was like the cat with the cream!

We reached the base, showed passports and papers and were eventually led upstairs into the operations room of the UN camp. It was situated in a school where murals remained on the walls from happier days when these rooms resounded with laughter from children.

The Major in charge was polite and business-like. Offering tea first, he explained the area we were entering had been under heavy fire, and directed us to the beginning of the 'Triangle' route, adding us as new players to what they called 'the theatre.'

This route started on a flat plain where brightly coloured, wild flowers waved in the light breeze. A few cows were grazing peacefully and I wondered what all the fuss had been about.

Both Jenny and Paul were in good spirits after a first class early lunch at the base. They were happy to be making some real headway. It wasn't long before the plains gave way to hills and the hills gave way to steep mountain tracks. Although the army was constantly maintaining these routes, Bluebell still had to wrestle with deep ruts and potholes.

She had a very low undercarriage, so there was very little room for mistakes. It would only take a moment's lack of concentration on Paul's part and Bluebell could lose her exhaust or, worse still, a hole could be smashed in her sump.

We turned a hairpin bend. Bluebell's nose was facing up to the sky at an acute angle. "Surely she won't be able to pull this heavy load up there!" I said.

Immediately Paul double de-clutched, accelerating so as not to lose any momentum. Bluebell spluttered, the dear old lady pulled her heart out for us as she slowly and laboriously crawled up the steep, rugged track. Paul patted her dashboard in appreciation. Our love and admiration for this old girl was growing by the minute.

The surge of adrenaline the struggle had generated was just what we needed to keep us going for what should have been a twelve-hour drive over some of the roughest mountain tracks in Bosnia. The UN had done an excellent job keeping the paths clear, but anything less than tarmac for dear old Bluebell put her in danger of seizure. Her springs creaked with every bump and pothole.

The elderly lady graciously made her way forward where the big sixteen tonners had pioneered the route. After about five hours in the warm sunshine we were beginning to feel we were the only people left travelling in the area. The only other living creatures in sight were the occasional goat and an odd cow or two.

I repeatedly checked the map as a wrong turn in this terrain could have dire consequences. In the wing mirror we delighted girls noticed a UN vehicle coming up on Bluebell's rear. They drew up level with us and to help relieve the monotony we threw a few sweets across from Bluebell's open window into the young men's cab. Delighted to see females still in existence, the soldiers immediately interpreted the gifts as an invitation to stop and chat

"How are you off for diesel?"

"Oh! We're OK thank you. We've half a tank," replied Paul.

"Well, if you like, we'll fill you up from our tank and we have a Jerry-can we'll also fill for you to take." Little did we realise the significance of this gift of fuel at the time.

Old Bluebell did her best to climb the extreme upward gradients as we continued to pick our way carefully around the boulders.

After eight hours of solid, concentrated driving through a second mountain range, we turned a sharp bend to find ourselves on the tail of a convoy we had seen sight of earlier. This line of about twenty trucks had been held up as one of the lorries had managed to slide over the edge and a great deal of effort was going into retrieving it.

"I imagine the military will not be too pleased to lose one of their wagons over the edge of a mountain, but at least it will give us a chance to take a breather," Paul mused, happy to relax at someone else's expense for a change.

The long hours of intensive journeying over the bumpy tracks had become quite tiring and tedious. The only thing which kept me going, was the anticipation of the expression on the hospital director's face when, God willing, we would arrive with the five incubators, held safely deep in the heart of Bluebell. I remembered well the needs of the pregnant lady we had met on a previous trip, who had received three bullets in her tormented body. She was the reason why we were making this trip. For her sake we would put up with all the discomfort in the world, for in a matter of hours we hoped to be at her side. This wonderful thought warmed me through and through.

After several hours in the dusk of evening the convoy in front stopped and to Paul's surprise, the officer in charge came up to the cab window. "Would you mind going right to the back of the convoy?" he said. "There's a lot of sniper fire in this area. We're going to put on our bullet-proof vests and drive through as fast as we can. If you can keep up, all the better. But, you must understand, we will be going through check points and if you get stopped, then you are on your own!"

"That's straight enough. Thank you for that at least!" I said politely, if not a little sarcastically. "It looks like they think we will be on our own again! He clearly knows nothing about Angels," I commented.

With their headlights on full beam, the convoy pulled away at top speed. Thankfully we were now on tarmac and Bluebell found it well within her ability to keep up. We were feeling very proud of her, when a single-decker bus pulled out in front of us from a side street. Many burnt out houses lined the route and people were trying to flee the area and this bus had probably slipped into the convoy to secure protection. "Look at that lucky so and so!" I thought. Then, said just as quickly, "Sorry Lord! I'm sure that bus is just where you want it to be!"

The words were no sooner out of my mouth than lights flashed ahead.

"Checkpoint coming up Paul! Don't look right! Don't look left! Just look straight ahead!" Out of the corner of my eye I could see the single-decker bus being ordered over. The guards complete with AK47 machine guns in hand were boarding it.

"Come on Paul! Don't stop now. Go through!" The way ahead, opened before us just like the Red Sea parted for the Israelites. In that instant the bus had become a shield to enable Bluebell and her crew to pass through the checkpoint safely.

I looked down at the dashboard. The fuel tank was half full. "Lord if you had not given us the gift of fuel earlier, we would have been out of diesel right in the middle of this!" Sinking back into my seat with a broad smile plastered all over my face, a sense of peace came over me. "Lord, I would rather have you than all the bullet-proof vests in the world. Thank you."

The convoy, having gone its own way was by now tucked up in camp for the night. Bluebell was on her own but still grinding forward after eighteen hours motoring. In the darkness ahead we could see a lorry parked broadside across the road. It just looked so odd. An evil, sinister atmosphere prevailed and I immediately responded to my primitive survival instincts. "Paul, turn this lady around, the UN base is only about two miles back. Enough is enough for one night!" Paul needed no prompting, as he also sensed something was very wrong.

Although the actual area we were in was very dark and quiet, the skyline behind was vivid red with the fierce glow from burning buildings.

It took all of my feminine wiles and much gentle persuasion for the UN Commander to agree to let Bluebell and her weary passengers into the camp. We were grateful for the camp beds and showers but most precious of all, Bluebell received a welcome drink of diesel by lining up with her big brothers.

It was one of the guards on duty who suggested that the road where the lorry was positioned broadside was in fact mined. Many of the Muslim houses had been burnt down that night and the occupants taken away by their enemy in full view, and only twenty yards from the UN entrance. Under their mandate all the soldiers could do was to stand by and helplessly watch these appalling scenes.

Despite the closeness of the horror of the war going on around us, I felt quite uplifted the following morning because maybe today we would be arriving at the hospital, our adopted people.

The only thing so far which was causing me a problem was my concern for the brakes. Because of their constant use they were burning and starting to smell during the descent of any slight incline. The smell from them was making me feel uneasy.

"Paul, use the air brakes. She won't last the journey at this rate," was my constant cry.

Paul seemed quite rattled at my suggestion, but I chose to ignore his hostile vibrations. Reaching for the flask I tried to give him a drink to soften his staring gaze.

Bluebell rolled from side to side as she got caught in some deep ruts made by heavy armoured vehicles.

"Careful Paul! Watch that boulder!" He braked hard then stopped. Bluebell's springs gave a screech of exasperation.

"That was close," grimaced Paul, "It looks like we are going to have to move that one," referring to a giant boulder in our path. The words had no sooner left his mouth than Jenny sprang into action. This sixty-nine year young lady was bending down and heaving for all she was worth in the full heat of the day. Triumph! The rock succumbed to her determined efforts and rolled to one side. This was Samson stuff, and soon I was patting Jenny's arm in appreciation. I felt a little ashamed of my own reluctance to let my back take any sort of strain, but knew if I did the price could be too much.

The hours passed slowly, and we were beginning to feel the strain of the hot sun as our minds and bodies became more and more tired. We had almost completed the 'Triangle' route, which, at Bluebell's sedate pace, had taken five gruelling hours. When suddenly, CRUNCH! A heavy scraping sound brought us all into sudden alertness. Bluebell had hit a boulder but we thought she seemed to have survived the impact.

We drove on and approached a small town, not really wishing to stop and check Bluebell. We wound our way around the narrow bends, Paul doing his best to avoid the lunatic local militia drivers who seemed to hold life on the roads as a very cheap commodity.

The whole atmosphere was uncomfortable and tense. The presence of evil in the air was so strong it was almost tangible. You could have cut it with a knife.

"Which way?" Paul was asking as we approached a 'T' junction.

"I'm not sure Paul, but turn left and we'll ask these men." I should have known better.

The groups were local army personnel, sitting waving guns in the air, laughing excitedly and clearly high on drink.

"Which way Zenica?" With roars of laughter, they pointed left, the way Bluebell was facing. "Hmmm!" I thought, trying not to be judgmental. Suspiciously, but following instructions, we turned left, took a right hand fork, which became gradually but continually more narrow the further we travelled.

The further we went the more obvious it became we had been deceived.

"Stop, Paul. There is no use continuing. We are obviously going in the wrong direction!"

"But I can't turn here!" He said quite flushed in the face, looking over the edge at the thirty metre drop, centimetres away from Bluebell's wheels.

"Paul, you're going to have to. I'll get out and watch the wheels so you don't go over the edge." As soon as I was on the ground, I saw we were in big trouble. Bluebell had been leaving a trail of thick, black oil. The worst possible thing had happened.

"She'll run out of oil before we can get to the next base," Paul stated quite categorically. "This is no place for an aid lorry to break down," he reasoned. "This food on board will well outweigh the value of our lives. Wouldn't those men back there like to have the contents of old Bluebell?"

Paul was careful in his manoeuvres and, as he was negotiating the tight space, I noticed the local militia watching us. A man with a walkie-talkie was clearly describing the scene.

"Let's get out of here!" I urged as Paul skilfully swung Bluebell round for the last time on the narrow path, we were at least now able to go in the right direction.

We found our way out of the town without too much trouble, loss of time, and hoped that we were heading in the right direction to the base.

"How much oil is left? Will it last out and get us there?" Paul didn't answer. He was not hanging about but pushing the old lady for all she was worth.

"There's a Warrior up ahead, Paul! We can't be too far away now!" True enough, there in front we could see the UN compound. The big white iron gates were closed protecting the columns of huge, heavy, armoured personnel carriers.

Approaching the main entrance, Bluebell limped quietly to a halt as we waited for permission to enter. Her outpourings became embarrassing. I blushed and was not amused by Bluebell's ungracious display. It was a bit like the breaking of the waters of a pregnant woman!

After being instructed in the rules and regulations I signed the official visitors' register. Only then were we allowed to enter the compound. Bluebell could hold out no longer, and proceeded to disgorge all the thick black oil from her entire sump, leaving a trail all the way from the main gate into the large, factory workshop.

Soldiers came rushing over with trays of sand to try to minimise the damage, but they were too late! Bluebell had truly left her mark on the British Army forever! This old girl would need a full hysterectomy. It seemed her weight bearing days were over.

For two days Paul and an army sergeant called Les worked relentlessly, as specialist surgery was required on Bluebell. The hole in her sump was thankfully repairable. It turned out she'd had a miscarriage, however there were still problems with her postoperative condition. The two men toiled side-by-side in a deep pit, first in extreme heat and then deep into the night.

Finally, the moment of truth! Bluebell, now off the respirator, roared into life, her heart was again beating, but oil was still pouring out of her womb. The gasket had not been stitched correctly, which meant the whole operation needed to be repeated. The two surgeons were exhausted and disappointed.

"Sorry, Jacqui; I'll keep on working but I don't think we'll make it in time to leave with the morning convoy."

There was nothing for it but to make the best of a bad job. Jenny and I would just have to amuse ourselves for another day. Whilst Paul continued working we had little trouble listening to the experiences of the war with the men in the lower ranks.

On hearing our intention to continue to travel over the 'Diamond' route the following day, a young sergeant bowed his head. Slowly, shaking it from side to side, he whispered,

"Lady, we went to retrieve the bodies of two Italians who were killed. There were four drivers, two escaped and were wandering in the mountains for two days, finally finding their way here, exhausted and in a terrible state. The other two..." his voice trailed off. He shook his head again as he recalled the dreadful sight. Now looking me straight in the eyes, "Lady, if you saw what they did to those men, what those bodies looked like, I am sorry," raising his voice, "then you would just not go any further."

I turned my body to the sun's rays, using it's warmth to prevent his words penetrating my inner being. I shrugged my shoulders and turned away asking to be excused.

'*Lord, it's no use listening to the seed of doubt. I can only listen to you. We have come this far, we need you to guide us.*' I rested back against the seat, soaking up the warmth, allowing God's creation to feed me in a deep way.

As time passed, Paul was delighted and relieved to report that Bluebell was fully recovered from her emergency operation.

"Bless you. Come and have a hot shower, then we'll have a good meal together," I said. Whatever is said about our British Army there is one thing which is indisputable. They make the most wonderful custard and, if possible, one needs to leave room for seconds of their lump-free creation.

"OK, you girls, what have you been up to today while I've been slaving under a hot lorry?" Paul was asking as Jenny and I looked sheepishly back in return.

"Well, it's like this. We've had a wonderful day with the boys, playing on a tank and having our photos taken. At least, that was the good bit. The bad bit was they told us about the Italians being shot but, it's no subject for the dinner table."

Not far into the meal we were joined by a large group of Overseas Development Agency drivers. They had nine 'heavy duty monsters' out in the compound, full of bulk food destined for Zenica.

"What time will you be leaving in the morning?" I enquired.

"We're under orders not to go any further, the fighting's too bad. We'll take this load back tomorrow."

I felt disappointed at the loss of aid for the people, especially as we were told that they were being paid £700 each to drive the lorries to deliver it. However I decided to put that resentful thought behind me and tuned back into my inner spirit.

'*So many warnings! Have I misheard you God, or is the enemy of my soul trying to distract us by sowing the seed of doubt?*'

"Go back, it's not worth it," their leader was saying.

'*Gosh! If they think that, and they know the difference they could make with nine lorries of food, then what right have I to risk three lives to deliver our little offering?*' I wrestled silently with this question as Paul and Jenny talked, laughed and shared some of Paul's light-hearted jokes.

I disappeared into my little corner upstairs where I had made my 'home' amongst the filing cabinets in the interpreter's office. We had two army issue camp beds between three people, one chair and a small table, which substituted as my dressing table in the mornings. This night, it was to be my altar.

"Lord, show me the way. We are available. We are available for you. We just want to be in your will." I sank back into the quiet of my own heart. It was still and peaceful.

"Yes, Lord, it is OK. We will go forward as planned in the morning and just trust you for everything, whatever may happen."

The one thing I was sure of: something big must be going to happen as our faith was certainly being tested!

CHAPTER 11

Ashamed

Next morning a news reporter approached us in the UN camp. "Are you going out today? Which way are you heading?" He addressed his questions to Paul who was checking Bluebell's water. Hardly giving Paul time to answer, he continued, "I'm going to Sarajevo but will be calling into Vitez for an escort."

"We are passing Vitez en route for Zenica. Maybe we could travel together?" Paul was asking.

"Yes, it looks as if they will give us a Warrior escort from the 'Picnic Area.'" (The army's name for the rendezvous area, before the most dangerous section.) The reporter was driving an armour-plated Range Rover and once on the road, wasted no time, in spite of the fact I had suggested Bluebell might not be able to keep up with his pace.

It was only minutes before we were out of the relative safety of the army compound and onto the dusty Diamond route. Bluebell bumped and groaned over the pitted track as her springs were stretched to their limits once more. Listening to her, one would think she would break in half at any moment, but this was God's tool, so I tried to quiet my thoughts.

The Warriors were already in position waiting for us at the 'Picnic Area' as the Land Rover drove straight past them. The huge army vehicles remained stationary.

"Paul, weren't they supposed to escort us through this next bit? Because if they were – then they aren't. We are on our own again and this is no place to be alone!" In the best of situations, I found the whole process of travelling compared well with my most unsettling nightmare. I wondered if others experienced such a degree of fear whilst driving.

We approached a particularly difficult stretch of road through the woods and I couldn't but help think of the poor Italians and their awful fate. This must have been the place where it happened, rocks on one side, woods the other, a perfect hi-jack position. The reporter's vehicle was wasting no time as if he too sensed the increased danger.

Jenny was awake for once and fully aware of the danger as Bluebell continued to bounce from side to side. She sat silently, not murmuring one word of protest. I held her hand for our mutual comfort as our eyes darted into every shadow amongst the trees.

"Jenny, I may find you a pain in the backside at times, but there is no doubting your courage," remarked Paul lovingly.

I started to sing. "Jesus, Name above all names." The other two joined in willingly, as the Holy Spirit moved upon our frail minds and calmed our fears.

From out of my heart, words were now forming in my mind as my inner voice began to speak. I reached for my pen to scribble on the back of an envelope. 'Do not fear man who would seek to take your flesh life, but fear God who will one day judge your time on earth.' "Yes, Lord, thank you for the reminder."

We were all relieved when we had come through the mountains and reached Vitez, where we flashed Bluebell's eyes as our reporter companion pulled into the barracks and gave cheery thumbs up sign. I imagined he was as relieved as we were to be through that section. It was true, the actual physical going forward into the unknown was being done half in naivety and half in blind faith, but for us faith was something we needed to exercise on a daily basis in order to grow.

At no time during the following hours drive on to Zenica did we feel able to relax our vigilance. In every shadow there seemed to lurk the manifestation of evil. Most of the buildings were destroyed, one house exposing an empty fridge and the shop safe which had both been looted.

Every few yards the roads were a mass of crumpled tarmac where grenades and shells had destroyed all the day to day normality of living. There was a single-decker bus on which every traveller had been killed, which we had seen on the news in England. I wondered where the people of the deserted villages we had passed through were now. Had they fled? Were they able to flee?

Further on, an odd group of children played with hand made wooden rifles, re-enacting the horrific scenes which they had lived through, which by now had become part of their normal lives. Many people had been burned alive huddled together whilst hiding in cellars; their supposed places of safety became their very tombs.

It was with relief that we turned on to the final stretch leading to Zenica, a town now surrounded by enemy forces on every side, a place sinking with the sheer weight of many thousands of homeless people. The excitement was mounting in me and I could hardly wait to see the hospital director's friendly face.

When we arrived the hospital was bursting with patients, many lying on blood-covered broken trolleys in the main reception area. Doctors and nurses showed all the signs of having worked night and day, each with their own personal story to hold in a breaking heart.

The hospital director welcomed us with open arms, hardly able to believe his eyes. He was feasting on our smiling faces. "Welcome! Welcome, brothers!" he seemed to say with every gesture, his hand frequently touching our arms as if needing reassurance himself we were really there!

He showed us into his office for refreshments. Immediately an interpreter was called for, as we wasted no time catching up on all the news.

"How is 'my lady'?" I enquired. The director's eyes dropped.

"The lady you speak of, Jasmina, her baby was born two days ago." I waited, holding my breath, "but it died early this morning."

"Oh Lord!" my heart sank. "Where is she? Can we go to her?"

"Yes, we will take you right away, but she doesn't know yet that the baby is dead."

Thinking about the bag that Helen had packed in England for her, I realised that we must take out the baby things, but Jasmina must still know that Helen and the family are there for her, especially at this time. I searched for the letter and photograph beckoning to the interpreter as we were led through the endless corridors of human suffering. Victims were either sitting on long benches, hobbling about on crutches or groaning on broken stretchers or planks of wood.

As we reached her bed, 'my lady' recognised us instantly. Tentatively I bent over, desperately trying to control my own emotions.

"My baby, my baby. You see my baby?" Holding back my tears and choosing my words carefully, I managed to whisper, "Your baby is in a good place. We have come to show you that you are so special."

I knew this lady was about to be used by God to focus our minds and energies. I wanted so much to love her better that I just reached out my arms and enveloped her with all my being. Tears ran down both our faces as we embraced and held each other tightly.

Reaching for the letter, I tried to find some composure and see through my own tear filled eyes, to enable me to justly share Helen's love. The letter was full of best wishes for the mother and the new baby, so less than skilfully I edited the text as I read it aloud, trusting it would be some time before Jasmina would be able to get someone to translate it in full for her. My voice continued to break as Helen's love reached out into this lady's pain. We were all one in the suffering. Silently I prayed in tongues for her emotional and physical healing, asking God to come and do a work of grace.

'*Lord don't let this baby's short life and this mother's pain be wasted,*' I prayed silently.

Exhausted, I tried to pull myself together having taken on board the pain of these dear souls in the hospital. Feeling at collapsing point under the emotional and spiritual weight, again I simply prayed.

'*Jesus, I am bringing these pains to you for your healing, please cover them and heal in a mighty way for your name's sake, Amen.*' Being with Jasmina had not been an easy experience but leaving her was even worse.

We wandered past an open door to one of the male wards; a nurse called us inside. There, lying on a bed was an elderly man, totally paralysed from the neck down. His eyes reached over to me as the nurse explained that Paul had prayed with that same patient on the Christmas trip. The nurse was now asking if we would both have a word of comfort with him. Paul joined me and we drew strength from each other. Far from us serving him, the man was serving us as a couple. The love between we three at that moment was electric and I savoured our brief contact as we all shared a special time in our heavenly Father's arms.

After receiving much needed refreshment, the hospital director's thoughts turned to the grave question he was holding in his heart.

"Jacqui, Paul…" he pleaded through an interpreter, "I would not ask you this if there were any other way." He went on, his voice trailing almost to a whisper. "You know I would not ask if it were not necessary, but could you go back to Zagreb and get us some more drugs? We have no anaesthetic, no X-ray film, and no morphine." His voice became more urgent. "We have not had any supplies for seven weeks. No one has been able to get through to us. You are our only hope. I will give you the necessary introductions to people who will help."

Our hearts sank with tiredness. For us Zagreb was a week's drive away and, at that moment, I was sure neither of us could face those mountains again. Our nerves were at breaking point. *'Oh Lord! What are you asking? What are you saying?'*

I pulled my body up to full height then looked our friend directly in his eyes.

"You know there is nobody else in central Bosnia who could ask this of us, but you. We will need at least two days to unload and feed the refugees in the school, but I know I speak for the others, for you our friend, anything."

After we unloaded the few medical supplies which we had brought, the local T.V crew on hearing we were at the hospital came to give us a video, filmed on our last trip. It was only later that we were to learn the significance of this gesture.

As we all walked slowly through the large hospital foyer led by men in white coats, I felt uncomfortable, being reminded of an occasion in my childhood when the governors processed through the school amongst us, the 'little people'.

Not happy to receive the elitist mantle, I was very relieved when a man who had been waiting for our appearance pulled me away and asked if we would take a letter back to England. It was amazing that, after so little time it seemed as if the whole of Zenica knew we had arrived! Receiving it I smiled at his initiative in coming to the hospital to find us. He tried to hang on to my arm, and not wishing to be impolite, I tried to reassure him. "I'm sorry, please excuse us because we must go and feed our family in the school, but, we will deliver your letter in England, I promise."

We bade the hospital director goodbye with the promise we would do our best to make it back to Zagreb and return with his urgent supplies. How much this man had become a part of our lives!

The school was only ten minutes drive away and as soon as Bluebell arrived, so did the crowds. It seemed the children were everywhere – even hanging from dear old Bluebell's wing mirror ears! A tall young man called Ricki, who was himself a refugee, was there to interpret for us.

Everyone had a good laugh at our dusty state. Some of the more elderly women shook their heads, sorry we had arrived in such a dusty condition.

"Come on! The sun is shining and we have wonderful surprises for you!" I called from my perch, standing high on Bluebell's running board. I produced about two hundred letters. One by one we called out the names, there were hands out stretched, kisses of appreciation and tears of joy as the lucky ones received the loving messages from family in England.

In amongst the excitement, Paul and I noticed a woman who by this time, was on her knees on the hard pavement, kissing and hugging her letter with tears of joy streaming down her face. We knew her to be a strong woman of great character. She was tragically cut off from her daughter, who thankfully was by now safe in England. As if compelled we pushed through the crowd, fell to our knees and shed tears of joy with her. For that moment the world stopped. Calm spread across the waiting crowd. The frame froze. Everyone's eyes were drawn to the cameo of oneness.

Jolted back to the task in hand by the sound of a car horn, I whispered. "Come on Paul, we've all the other letters to distribute!" There were the inevitable disappointed faces. The joys we brought to some seemed to highlight the disappointment and hurt of others. "Come on, Paul let's get some of the food boxes off for them."

"Jacqui, do you know what you're asking? We've not stopped for days. Can't we have a rest first?" But he knew better, nothing would stop me from finishing the job at hand.

Paul immediately arranged to have the food boxes passed through an open window of a downstairs classroom. We knew if we tried to pass the boxes through the main entrance hall, some of the boxes would go astray via the unscrupulous ones. So a human chain was made and everything was passed through the open window into the hands of appointed leaders.

There were seventeen classrooms in the school, some with thirty-five people in each. Many families were living together day and night in one classroom.

Once all the boxes were inside, we placed seventeen tables side by side to form a counter. We then emptied each box and sorted the food into some order. Jam, toothpaste, beans, sugar, flour and oil; all would be shared equally. Eventually there were seventeen tables completely full of every kind of gift one could imagine.

Now the big problem: how to get the aid safely into each classroom, through the dense wall of human need, which was by now, pushing and pulsating against the door?

"Ask for two representatives from each room to come in, one pair at a time," I suggested to the tall young interpreter. Ricki threw his hands in the air, exasperated at my naïve suggestion.

"Jacqui you don't understand! The minute we open that door there's going to be a stampede. The children are just going to get crushed. Some of them will wait patiently, but the others will grab everything they can."

"OK, the strongest men will have to guard the door from the inside, and then we will have to defend against the crowd."

Paul positioned men with their shoulders against the door. Ricki and I braced ourselves as they released the lock taking the full weight of the surging crowd. Some of the women at the front of the crowd were prepared with blankets, ready to carry the first loads away but, I realised they would struggle to get their heavy burdens back through the mass of human excitement.

"You!" I indicated, pointing at one strong man. "You please help these ladies." He shrugged his shoulders.

"Help? Who me? No way!" His response was easy to interpret. I waved my arms at him, now determined. "No help! No food!" My frustration was growing.

"Ricki tell these men, please tell them I mean business. If they don't co-operate – no food! No more letters! No next time!" They calmed a little. "Now tell them, *if* we can get this food distributed, then we have some shoes to share out." That seemed to please them, and they gave way for the women to enter the room and load their blankets.

Having solved the food distribution problem we finally laid out the shoes on the tables, which we hoped would also serve as some protection from the crowd.

'Maybe we can let them come in en-masse and sort them out for themselves…or maybe not!' I was turning this idea over in my mind

when the door burst open. In stormed a throng of sweaty, aggressive men each determined to get their hands on any shoes before their neighbours. The pressure of the heaving crowd pushed the arrangement of tables back into the only standing space available. To prevent myself from being crushed, I managed to scramble onto a desk. Desperately I grabbed a terrified child who was within my reach, just managing to save him from being trampled beneath the weight of the powerful, hostile mob. Men pushed the women and children aside, caring only about their own needs. Some men were grabbing handfuls of children's shoes, shoving them into their pockets. Anger welled up inside me but I was marooned on top of a table, helpless, and for a time I was ashamed to be part of the human race.

Within minutes the room looked like an old junkyard, nothing left but empty boxes and paper strewn everywhere. Ricki stood in shock and shame. After all, this was not representative of all the people, but it was still true to say that many came from greed and not the need. The battle inside me raged.

There had been little sense of satisfaction in the day's work, and as a way of lifting our spirits we decided to take a 'baby carriage' and some baby food to the orphanage. There were sixty-five babies there and some pregnant women who were the victims of rape. They had been attacked in full view of everyone in their own villages. Sickened to my stomach at the thought of how they were coping with their humiliating experience I pushed the thoughts out of my mind. "Come on you guys, a good cup of tea is the order of the day."

Thankfully at that moment, Zejna and Edo were there to gather up our aching bodies which were still feeling the ravages of the day.

CHAPTER 12

The Loaves and the Fishes

Early the following morning in Edo's flat, the lounge was filled with the smoke from Meho's cigarettes, and it wasn't long before Mujo arrived to compound the pollution. It was good to see the men again, and as they sat round the large coffee table, Zejna again acted as interpreter for us. They seemed anxious to tell of the desperate situation of their soldiers. Meho was extremely patriotic and eventually asked if Paul and I could bring food for the hungry soldiers.

Stunned and confused by his request, I felt I needed more information. Not wanting to take political sides or be guilty of neglecting to help the needy, I asked if we could be taken to meet the officers in charge. I knew this would help me to discern in my spirit what was right.

After a few phone calls it was arranged and we were taken on a conducted tour of the local barracks. It was totally run down and grimy with an atmosphere of defeat hanging over it.

"This is where the eighteen-year-olds are brought to be trained to fight," the mature man in charge told us. I imagined my eighteen-year old son, Richard, leaving home, maybe for the first time and finding himself in such a place. Even worse was the thought that he would then be expected to go out and kill, all within a matter of three weeks.

The armaments consisted of a few broken down tanks which looked as dilapidated as the place itself. Instinctively I wanted to do my sergeant major act and put extra discipline in, to tighten up the place, as I saw in the neglect the reflection of the rock bottom morale of a nearly defeated army.

I wanted to do what we could for these people, but still I wasn't sure if it was the right thing to do. We progressed over to the medical centre where a young man was being given attention for a severe wound in the calf of his leg. My stomach turned so my eyes veered involuntarily away.

Realising my mistake, I forced myself to look again to try to give the young man some support. Bless him, he had seen my reaction and had covered himself to save my embarrassment from my weakness. A small, sensitive gesture but typical of many we were meeting.

"Let's go, Meho! I have seen enough!" I said shaking my head despairingly, as we all made our way over to his car. Paul and Jenny were by this time both bending my ear with their differing opinions, each going on and on, but I needed space to make my own decision.

When we arrived back at the flat I wanted to separate myself away from the conversations and thankfully, having done this, it wasn't long before the answer became clear to me. After checking with Paul, I addressed Meho directly.

"Meho, I am now clear for myself, and speak on behalf of all the people who support us in England. Firstly, I want you to know we will do anything within the bounds of our moral code and within our power to help you or your family personally. We have looked deeply into your request, but we have decided the answer is... no. I am quite clear now. We are here to help war victims, not to aid the continuation of the war. If your men need feeding, then that is the responsibility of your government."

Meho was clearly shocked and disappointed but also seemed to respect my direct and concise answer. I continued, "Now, if there is anything we can help you with personally, please ask."

I could see there was a lot more he wanted to discuss with us. Zejna was very patient, working hard to interpret conversations between Meho, Paul and I.

"Jacqui, maybe you sell me Bluebell?" Meho enquired.

"Bluebell! Our lady! Why do you need her?"

"I need to go Italy to buy food and shoes for army."

The thought of leaving Bluebell in Bosnia would feel like leaving my legs behind. The mere suggestion had thrown me completely off balance. "Meho, if you need a lorry, send the money to England and we will buy you your own vehicle and bring it over for you quite legally."

I could see the right hand drive and the British plates would give Meho a moment's credibility at the checkpoints and those could just be the vital moments.

"OK I think about it!" Meho was saying, but I could see there was still more. "Jacqui, you help me get to Split? I get papers from police to travel. You go with me?"

"Now what's going on?" All my red alarm lights were flashing at once. Zejna interrupted.

"It's OK, Jacqui, I will be going with Meho to help him. We need to take a large van to carry food etc. and we will both be able to get special papers."

I searched Edo's face. He was quiet, a solid family man whom I respected and trusted. The question flashed through my mind, *'Lord, what could we be getting into?'*

"Meho, I want to help you, but I do not want to help you with anything illegal." There were laughs and smirks round the room.

Now I felt I should feel guilty for even having such a thought. Still I stood my ground.

"Tell me, Meho. What exactly do you want of us?"

"I need to get out of Bosnia. I haven't been able to get out for six months. My people need food. They need me to go."

"I see that," I found myself saying. "Then I will come in your van with you, and Zejna can go in Bluebell with the others, but please let's get one thing clear. I will not commit Paul or Jenny to take such a risk. I am only willing to make a personal commitment here, and that's only if Paul is in agreement."

I was acutely aware of Meho's devastating charm and his expertise at getting his own way and, whilst I may have wanted to help him, I could see no reason for the others to be involved in extra dangers on their way out of Bosnia.

"Meho, what papers will you get?"

"I get good papers. I know many people. Nema problema! Nema problema!"

Everything is "No problem" in Bosnia. It's contagious. I smiled realising the reality behind his easy use of the expression.

"I'll tell you what we will do," I said, getting out the map. "Paul, Jenny and Zejna will travel this way," pointing out the route by which they had already come, which we knew to be as safe as possible in the circumstances. "I will travel with you with my British passport…this way!" Pointing to the nearer side of Bosnia through the Mostar route where the UN wagon had been blown up. "Then we will meet here," pointing on the map. "But you need to know, actually, the only way through is, by the grace of God and prayer."

"Jacqui, nema problema!" he was saying again. "our soldiers watch our way."

"Yes," I smiled, "but what about your enemies? Who tells them to let us through?" I was trying to lighten the conversation.

Later, when I was re-running the plan in my mind, Edo cut through my thoughts.

"Jacqui," he smiled. "You did right to make the decision not to help the army directly." He was being his usual sweet, supportive self.

"The truth is Edo, I had no idea what our own mandate was until I was pressed to clarify it in my own mind, but now I am satisfied having done so."

After lunch with the family, I made my way back to the school alone. The whole atmosphere was, by now, much more relaxed. The people knew Bluebell was completely empty. I knew if they bothered to talk with me now it was because they wanted to share and not for what they could get. This was my recreation time, and I was growing to love this part of the ministry.

Narjia had made some fish shaped pastries for our lunch. I asked if she minded if I saved mine as I had a much better use for it. So after lunch, with fish in hand, I happily made my way back to the school. I knew my time with the families would be a blessed time. They were always so welcoming.

"Hi, Jacqui" "Jacqui, Jacqui!" the children would call out, some rushing up to hold my hand, others trying to get me to go into their room first.

Whenever I entered a room I did so in bare feet. This was their ground, sacred ground. These few feet per person represented their only status in the world. Each little area by each bunk bed was unique. There were odd bits of curtain hanging up, suspended by string. A few metal pots and pans peeped out from under the beds. I noticed a hand-drawn picture on the bottom of one bed. This picture had been sent by children from a school in England. But most of my pleasure came from the joy on the faces. Most faces were ingrained with hardship, but all lit up with smiles as we anticipated some precious time with each other.

In one room I was invited to sit on the only wooden chair. One lady rushed up with a hand-made pillow to put behind my back. She smiled, caught my hands in hers, then put her head down and kissed them gently. The people all moved in closer, finding a little space on the floor or on the edge of a bed on which to sit. They gazed expectantly at me, wondering what might come out of the paper bag I was holding.

"Where is Ricki? The tall boy!" I needed some help to communicate. Within a few minutes the young man appeared and offered his services again as interpreter.

Proudly I produced the fish which I had brought to them to share. Now they were puzzled, how could I make one small fish go round so many people?

"Ricki, please tell them I am very happy to be sharing this day with them. I would like to tell them a story about a small boy." They smiled in approval. I went on. "One day there was a big crowd gathered around Jesus as he taught. The people had travelled many miles and had no food. Thankfully, in the crowd was one small boy. He had five loaves and three fishes, just like this one." I held up my pastry fish. "Of course, there was not enough to feed everybody, but Jesus prayed and then instructed his disciples to feed the people from the gift offered. All were fed, and not only that but there were many baskets full of food left over.

Do you remember when we first came here we only had two bars of chocolate to share with you? Now we have been able to bring a lorry full of food. Can you see how God has honoured our faith and how much He loves you? Can you see how many people in England are reaching out to show love to you as a nation?" Now, getting quite excited, "Do you know people keep coming to our door with bags of food and they ask us to bring this food to Bosnia with their love?" Lowering my tones, "Will you please now see Paul and I are only the donkeys, carrying the gifts to you?" They smiled and I was happy. They had understood the point.

"Now Ricki, please tell them today is what's called, Good Friday."

"What is this Good Friday, Jacqui?" Ricki was asking.

"Good Friday was the day they crucified Jesus on the cross. Regardless of religious origins, we do worship the same God, Our Father in Heaven."

The message was relayed. "Please tell them, that the word of God teaches that, when Jesus Christ hung on the cross, He hung there that we might be forgiven.

He hung there for all the people of the world, who would *on faith,* believe in His great love and sacrifice for them. Ricki, please tell them, Jesus Christ died as payment for our sins." Ricki spoke, the room was still. "He wants to forgive each one of us and what's more, He wants *us* to forgive all those who have hurt us." That includes all the people who are still hurting your people."

Ricki wasted no time interpreting. "Jacqui, we do forgive. We have no problem forgiving if only," he paused, "if only they would stop killing us."

I understood his point and, although I did not realise it at the time, I now believe it was at that moment that God planted the seed of compassion in my heart for this young man. I believe to this day that at that moment this young man spoke his heart before God. God heard it and purposed His response for his life through us. I continued now very gently.

"Ricki, what do you think is the bottom line of Christianity? Didn't Jesus' death show us that He was prepared to die for all of mankind?"

"So what you are saying?" Ricki asked.

"Well, you see Ricki, as I figure it…anybody can take my flesh life in a moment… but nobody can touch my Soul or my Spirit. I believe, as crazy as it may sound, it is better to be the one to die for ones faith, rather than the one to do the killing. We don't have to worry about this world; it's the next we need to be concerned about. The Word of God says: 'For God so loved the world, that He gave His only begotten Son that who ever believes in Him shall not perish but have everlasting life'."

"So, are you saying Jacqui, that only Christians can have eternal life?"

"No, what I am saying is, when Jesus taught that everybody, regardless of physical birth, has to be born again, He was talking about a spiritual birth.

I am against the concept, which says that if you are born in England that automatically makes you a Christian, no that is a cultural relationship. No, Jesus taught that we need to have a spiritual birth and a personal relationship with God. You see, regardless of to whom we are born, we are still of the flesh from our mothers' wombs. Then when we realise we have actually failed and *see* that we need to be forgiven for our sins, and are prepared to ask God to forgive us. Then we are at the place where we can be born again, but this time it means, being born of and by the Holy Spirit of God. Jesus clearly taught that unless we are born again we cannot enter the Kingdom of God."

Silence fell across the room as the young man translated the message. The women nodded their heads in approval. They agreed. "Please, now let us pray together." They all stood up and we joined hands. My voice and heart went up to Heaven as I claimed peace for these precious souls in Jesus' name. They in turn prayed their prayers asking God to forgive them. We had the same Father. Now the Holy Spirit was moving that we could be as one in spirit through His Son, Jesus Christ.

The energy in the room was powerful. Words were not needed. We touched hands, smiled and nodded at each other. It mattered not that we did not speak the same language. We shared the same Father and for that moment, if only for that moment, we were one in Christ.

I made my way back towards the flats through the crowds of well wisher's and dragged my weary body back up the long, dark flights of stairs. The higher I climbed the more ugly the darkness became. I hated the dark! I hated the gloom! And what's more, I hated why these people were suffering!

CHAPTER 13

An Oasis

It's hard for us in England to appreciate what it really must be like to be trapped in a country surrounded by one's enemy, when you can't simply go and fetch food to feed your family. We have no comprehension of what it must feel like when families are separated and one is unable to reach them. The agony and frustration is hard to imagine, and I certainly did not quite appreciate what it must have felt like for Meho on this occasion.

He was a man used to getting things done and now he had to take the slenderest of chances to try and get out of his country, down roads probably used by him as a young man for courting. Most of the civilian population must be totally confused as to why they were being persecuted.

"What do they want us to do? Live on the moon?" Zejna murmured on countless occasions.

Meho at this time was using his influence to get papers to travel through Bosnia and Croatia but with very little certainty, as a Muslim, that he would not be slaughtered along the way.

Having visited 'our families' in the school, and given our promise that by the grace of God we would return to the hospital director, we were now ready to leave.

Meho drove a big, ugly, old van with me as passenger. Paul, Jenny and Zejna followed in Bluebell since they had elected to travel the same route, under firm instructions, that if any of us were held up in any way, the others were to go on.

The whole atmosphere was tense, but I was heartened when the officials at the early Muslim checkpoints seemed to have very genial conversations with Meho. He was clearly a very popular person and used his personality to the full.

The whole journey ran remarkably smoothly. Meho pointed out various landmarks along the way, including the convent where forty-two nuns had been murdered. The convent still showed the bullet holes and burnt remains of that dreadful night when the whole area was razed to the ground. It's hard to imagine what such a night would be like. Here was a whole nation where every person was scarred not only physically, but also with internal wounds.

The journey back across the mountains and through repeated scenes of devastation was no easier the second time. We now had the added pressure of fighting our tiredness. I imagined Paul's natural cheerful nature in the vehicle behind would be a blessing, knowing we all needed to continue to wrestle with the constant murmuring of our fears. In my case it wasn't just murmuring but down right screaming within my mind.

As we relentlessly wound our way down the steep mountain tracks, Meho managed to drive the vehicle perilously close to the edge, where there were many crumpled lorries, their occupants' fates probably sealed in an early grave.

Finally we approached the Croatian border and Meho was showing every sign of mounting tension and understandable apprehension. He had increased his speed and was chain smoking as his eyes darted continually from left to right. I checked in the wing mirror. Although Bluebell was still in sight, I was happy that the old lady was still quite a safe distance away, separated enough not to be associated with us.

Duly halting in front of the guards who stood in front of the barrier, Meho without a word handed over my passport.

"Not enough!" they gesticulated, "Your papers!" With another deep puff on his cigarette, he complied silently and handed over the newly acquired 'so called' pass. The guard looked him in the eye, every muscle in me went solid. Then as smoothly as possible he simply handed the papers back. We were through!

I didn't know how Meho contained himself but, as soon as we were out of sight of the border guards, he managed to fling his arms around me despite continuing to drive forward! He shouted almost at the top of his voice, "Big God! Big God!" How we rejoiced! Freedom never tasted so sweet!

We all shared in his elation by celebrating in a local coastline restaurant where Meho ordered the best fish on the menu. To say we shared his joy is not quite accurate. Zejna shared his joy. I however, squirmed in my chair as Zejna held an octopus eye in her fingers, ready to let it slide down her long slender throat. "Don't do it!" I squirmed, completely letting myself go, I was ready to dive out of the window into the sea below, had I been sure I would have landed in the water with the grace of Esther Williams, the movie star. "If you eat that thing I will never let you use my lipstick again!" I threatened.

After a well-deserved break I joined Paul and Jenny back in Bluebell. Meho and Zejna went their separate way to attend to their own business.

After hours of concentrated driving we were relieved to be off the mountains and travelling together again. Paul began to enjoy the freedom of tarmac under Bluebell's fine steering, and managed to underestimate his own tiredness. He simply missed a halt sign and pulled out, straight in front of a giant double tanker coming down hill at full speed towards us. Jenny and I screamed and hung on to each other. Paul, as usual, kept cool and accelerated harder, thus avoiding a horrible end for us all. The Grace of God had given him perfect timing.

"That was good wasn't it?" Paul proudly exclaimed. That did it! My frail nerves just snapped.

"What are you doing Paul?" I protested. "Just cool it. Let's not repeat that exercise, we may not be so lucky next time. You are driving like a maniac. I know you are tired. I know you just want to get this whole thing over with but, we are not going to get out of here if you continue in this way." I went on and on.

My words met hostile glances. His self-defence mechanism came into play, nothing I was going to say would help. The dividing line was drawn. Things between us proceeded down the spiral fast and soon we were at each other's throats. The more my words were met with denials, the more I went for the jugular. I was still trying to give Paul a warning about his own tiredness, and lack of reactions, but nothing I could say by this time would be taken on board.

"The fireworks in our cab are brighter than the Houses of Parliament on a Prime Ministers Question Time," Paul quipped in his dry humorous way, as a smoke screen rather than owning his own responsibility.

Poor Jenny must have thought she was in the middle of World War Three! But bless her, unbeknown to me, Jenny had begun to trust my judgment now a little better, and measure it against her own instinct for survival. For the first time I sensed Jenny was in agreement with what I was trying, unsuccessfully, to communicate to Paul.

For Paul, that only made it ten times worse. He flipped completely and now driven by his own anger, drove faster and faster. We hung on in there, desperately thinking what to do, and

I at the same time was trying to bite my tongue. There was nothing else for it.

"Stop this vehicle!" I ordered in no uncertain terms. "We can't go on like this, we must stop!"

The abrupt silence was overbearing. One could cut the atmosphere with a knife.

"Paul, you don't have the right to kill us, so please stop this lorry. We must stop and ask for forgiveness, you and I are both guilty, both at fault."

It was true to say nerves were shattered and bodies exhausted, so I asked Paul if he fancied a cup of tea as I reached for the flask of lukewarm water. I persisted more gently now.

"Paul, why don't you pull over and drink this? The few minutes stop will do you good." For whatever reason, at that very moment God had supplied the grace that I needed and stopping at that moment was to change the whole course of our lives.

Silently, and without resentment, Paul pulled Bluebell over on to some ground just outside a small, local shop, which happened to have a large forecourt. We had a short time of prayer, during which we asked our Heavenly Father to forgive us, cleanse us, and fill us with His Spirit. Now our Heavenly Father could take over and really start to move again in a miraculous way.

We sat quietly watching the world go by for a few moments and refreshing ourselves on the tepid tea, which only half resembled the blend our taste buds knew. We watched with interest each person emerging from the shop, particularly a big, burly man with dark hair who was unshaven.

Despite his broad smile, his face portrayed the hardships and concern experienced by every family man at this time. By his side walked a very clear skinned, very gentle in demeanour, young girl. She seemed about fifteen years old and appeared to be his daughter. First he looked at Bluebell's registration plates then up to the cab. On seeing himself being looked up and down, he approached with a big, friendly smile.

That smile made a connection and was to be the catalyst for a whole new chain of events. It wasn't long before he was telling us the girl was, in fact his daughter, and he had three other children. He went on to explain it was most difficult to try and keep body and soul together during these times, as everything was in short supply.

It was difficult to listen to him attentively, because of his broken English, and excitable manner as he communicated his anger about the cost of his purchase. The young girl was a lot easier to understand. She spoke much better English and tried to interpret for her father.

"My father says would you like to join us for tea at our home? It's not far away. We live up in that direction."
She pointed way up into the hills and mountains, beyond the rear of the shop. Maybe it was the sound of the word 'tea' or maybe because we had no more resistance in us, or maybe the purity of this young girl's face that gained our trust, but we were ready to follow anywhere.

Before we could think it through, the father was approaching us with gifts he had fetched from his car, bags of lavender and a little bottle of pure lavender oil. He indicated to us that we should tie the bags on the light switch on Bluebell's dashboard.

"It is good," he was saying, gesticulating in a broad manner reflecting the fullness of his character. My basic instinct and thought of English tea took over.

"Thank you, that would be most welcome. Shall we follow you?" I queried.

Paul laughed, "Do you know Jacqui, listening to you trying to communicate with that man," he paused, "well you are to languages what Churchill was to Woodbines!"

I picked up an imaginary flower. Now pulling off the petals, "He loves me, he loves me not, he loves me, he loves me not."

It wasn't long before we were following up a very steep hill, crawling at 10kph round three hairpin bends on our way out into what seemed like Outer Mongolia! After about ten minutes climbing at Bluebell's slow pace, the road flattened out and revealed, on our left, about six gun turrets, all with heavy guns in place, and all pointing the same direction over the mountains.

"You know, if we hadn't just prayed and got right before God, I would say to follow a strange man all this way into this area, would be a ridiculous thing to do. I have to believe God is leading us here, because He has a real purpose for our coming." The other two agreed as we each smiled at our own child-like faith, or utter stupidity!

At last we followed our guide, Zdravko, round a right hand turn, opposite a cemetery, on to a dirt track and minutes later our host was pulling in between large boulders and two small trees which formed the gateway to his unique home.

It is unlikely that any home in the world was like this one. Firstly, it was almost totally built by this man's own hands and, whilst it did not have too much in common with suburbia, it had an unmistakable charm of its own.

The children came running and lined up in order as Zdravko proudly presented them one by one. They were all delightful, the sort of children who would have made perfect actors for a T.V. series such as '*The Waltons.*'

Then, much to our delight he presented his wife. This lady approached with great self-confidence and outstretched arms. I felt I could just fall into them and she would protect me forever. Maria, the wife, was Dutch. She could never be described as pretty but had a fascinating aura of sensuality. Her greying hair was very cleverly used to disguise one false eye. She was slim and attractive in a most unusual way.

It took only a few minutes conversation for me to know we were of the same ilk. She was my sort of woman. I could not believe this experience we were all having. One minute Paul and I were at each other's throats, then Lord, you brought us here!

The children were quick to show Jenny the family dog, Bella and her three puppies, whilst Paul went back to Bluebell to find a box of sweets for them.

This home fascinated me. The woodwork, considering Zdravko built it, was truly wonderful. There was a large fireplace surrounded by many shelves with books on everything from psychology and family health to homeopathy. On the far wall were two giant charts of the human body, exposing all the key organs. These I found intriguing and went over to look at them, but then I was led to the long, oak, family table that seated about eight people without crowding.

Soon jugs of tea and coffee were boiling on the wood burning stove in the chaotic, open plan kitchen. The design was not to my own ordered taste, but I loved the whole feel of the functional family home these interesting people had created.

It wasn't long before Zdravko had asked if Paul, Jenny and I would like to stay the night and, although it was still only about 5 p.m. we willingly accepted the invitation.

We wanted to know more about this fascinating family. Before long every subject from the politics, the hardships of the war to religion had been discussed. We were, of course, only getting the measure of each other, and whilst Zdravko and I were soon to find we weren't always in agreement, Maria and I found we had much in common.

Nevertheless, Zdravko and Maria were both fascinated by what we were doing. Zdravko used every small incident we described as an excuse to cross himself in front of his imaginary altar! In a matter of two hours his moods had frequently swung fervently from one extreme to another. In my heart I registered a warning signal but, at the same time, had no trouble in immediately loving this extraordinary, eccentric character.

The evening passed without incident which was quite surprising as Zdravko's gesticulations became more and more exaggerated with every glass of wine he drank. He was a man who clearly liked to be the king ruling in his own kingdom in a firm, explosive, yet I could see, loving way.

Whatever this man was bringing up in me, I was sure about two things. Firstly, he was a giant with a character that encompassed both the lion and the lamb. Secondly, behind every man there is a woman, and in Maria's case she had a full life's work offering her own gifts wisely and, at the same time keeping her place firmly behind her husband in support. I loved her for it. Before leaving to catch the ferry and after a most precious time of relaxation with the couple, they gave us a huge, hand made wooden rosary, a most beautiful gift.

The next chess piece came into our possession as we were on the ferry from Split travelling north to Rijeka the following day. Soon after we boarded, Paul, whilst up on deck, began to talk to some Irish aid workers, who said they were supported by some nuns back home in Ireland.

I thought it would be rather nice to acknowledge them by giving them the rather large wooden cross and oak beads which Maria and Zdravko had given us. I felt such a gift was better placed in a convent. After explaining the personal value of the gift, I asked if they would like to take it back to the nuns as an acknowledgement from the people of Croatia.

The gift was graciously received and nothing more was thought about it until one of the same aid workers approached the group at the dining table much later.

"We have a single mattress in the back of our van and wondered, if you would like it?" I was a little stunned by the question.

"What a strange gift," I remarked to Paul out of their earshot.

"Well, Lord, if you think we need a single mattress, then we must need a single mattress. OK throw it on board!" Grateful, but without any understanding as to why it was given, the single mattress was loaded into the back of Bluebell. So pleased were we for a few hours of relative safety, we all proceeded to enjoy the deep red sunset over the harbour and celebrated by singing choruses seated in a quiet corner of the upper deck.

Before addressing any sleeping arrangements, Jenny took the initiative and simply curled up in her arctic weight sleeping bag in a small space under some stairs. We knew she could sleep on a clothesline but nevertheless in view of her sixty-nine years she often put us to shame in this respect.

Thankfully, Paul and I had become quite familiar with most of the crew by this time and as there was a shortage of cabins, one of them asked if we would like to use his bunk for the night whilst he was on duty. We felt like cats that had got the cream and, we even had completely clean sheets. So on waking early next morning, I was pleased to use the time to write our kind sailor friend a note of thanks and encouragement.

After disembarkation it took just another few hours to drive from the port back to Zagreb in Croatia where we were greeted with huge, warm hugs from Ruza. Mascara now on, she looked a new woman and the flat was spick and span. She had a new, mischievous air about her, further enhancing her fun personality.

I was seeing a new side to her and one I could fully appreciate. She seemed the type of woman few men would have the strength to resist, clearly in this mood she would get her way in most situations.

Meho was expected in a few minutes, having completed his business and travelling by a different route for the last part of the journey. With his dynamic personality, it seemed a very full house when he arrived, yet at no time did I see his mantle slip. He seemed to remain distant, except where Deni was concerned. There was much discussion about Deni's future and a lot of talk as to whether, for his own safety he could go back to England with us. Ruza clearly did not want to leave, but there was nothing she wouldn't do for her sons.

I had perceived Deni's way of manipulating his mother into getting his own needs met. As a young man, Deni needed the lines of discipline to be made quite clear, any blurring of the lines left him able to manipulate his mother. Clearly, Meho had always been the authority and Deni respected and loved him. I also knew Deni would have done anything to protect his mother but, as he was not yet a man, there could still be playful friction between them. I committed in my heart to staying close to both of them, simply trusting to be there when needed.

Deep in thought I became aware of strange music coming from the lounge. Popping my head round the door to enquire what it was, I saw Paul viewing the video that had been made about our last trip to the hospital (the film the local T.V. crew in Zenica had given to us). Suddenly horrific scenes appeared on the screen. The crew had spliced, in the centre of the film, pictures of some of the atrocities that had happened very recently in central Bosnia.

I looked at the screen, hardly able to believe my eyes. Trays of men's genitals were being held up for all to see. They had been ripped off young men whilst others had been tortured in equally horrendous ways. A pregnant woman had her womb cut open, so 'they' could bet on the sex of the unborn baby.

Feeling physically sick and horrified I left the room unable to control my emotions.

'*What are you doing walking away Jacqueline?*' I berated myself. '*This is reality. This is really happening. This is what is happening in Bosnia now, today! This is what it is all about.*' My heart was a mixture of anger and hurt, '*Lord what is going on? Why did they give us this film? What is it you want us to see?*' As usual there were more questions than answers.

Gingerly I returned to the room and forced myself to look again. Piles of broken bodies were shown on the screen, some, although their limbs were blown off, were still alive lying in pools of their own blood. These were the pictures the media in England were not showing. These people clearly wanted the true story to be told. '*And, Lord, you wanted us to see the reality, but Lord, please show me what you would have us do to serve you and these people?*'

I met Meho in the hallway. "Jacqui, you take Deni and Ruza with you, your home?"

"That's fine but will they come?" I asked. "And will our government allow it?" After a few phone calls to the Embassy to check, it appeared as they both had Croatian passports they could go to England as our guests.

We had yet to return to the hospital back in central Bosnia, so it was agreed Ruza and Deni would fly to England from Zagreb airport with a covering letter of guarantee, which I wrote and signed. Meho would pay for Ruza and I offered on behalf of our supporters to pay for Deni. There had been a lot of soul searching by the family to decide what the best thing was for Deni, because of what seemed like his absolute intent to get killed by going off and fighting for his country in this terrible war.

As I had just seen on the video what dreadful things they were doing to each other, I had no doubt if Deni and Ruza would go to our home in England it would probably save Deni from eventually being killed. The decision was made! Tomorrow they would leave with just one suitcase, I made the necessary arrangements.

'Isn't it amazing,' I thought, shaking my head in despair. Dwight L Moody wrote: 'A great many people are trying to make peace, but that has already been done. God has not left it for us to do: all we have to do is enter into it.' So why don't we?

With two good nights sleep behind us, we set off to find the warehouse in Zagreb to load the life saving food and medical supplies onto Bluebell's back for the long, arduous journey back to the hospital. The warehouse was full up to the ceiling with food and supplies, yet people were dying for lack of the life saving items getting through. After much discussion with the lady doctor in charge and wrangling with the customs officials, Bluebell was loaded for her most vital effort yet. Fully loaded, and in this political climate the journey if all went well, could take anything up to a week.

We weren't on the road long before we discovered the old lady was having some difficulty staying on her feet, as the uneven distribution of weight in her load was causing her to be light on the steering. Paul was doing his best but, as the hours and miles began to mount, I realised the load would have to be re-packed if we were going to make it over those dreaded mountains again.

We didn't make the first UN base until about 2pm the following day and to be safe we needed a top up of fuel as well. Having obtained special permission from the Commander we pulled over to the giant petrol tanker to refuel. Reluctantly, Paul agreed to stop and look at the weight distribution problem at the same time.

"Come on let's unload and reload Bluebell," was my hearty suggestion, but given the excessive temperature the words from my mouth were understandably not received too enthusiastically by Paul. I felt that, given the difficulty of the fighting ahead, we should do all in our power to eliminate every unforeseen possibility and danger. This included looking at Bluebell's springs.

It turned out one of the rubber bushes on her springs had completely worn away. This explained why she had been groaning under the excessive weight! Having tried, and failed, to get help from the 'top brass,' we did what we should have done in the first place. "If you want any real help from the UN start at the bottom and work up," was one of Paul's perceptions and in this instance he was absolutely right.

One young British soldier came to our assistance. His name was unknown as he laboured under Bluebell in the excessive heat. He may never realise the gift he gave that day, because many long arduous hours later, after we had battled again with the mountains and the heat, we were stopped at a checkpoint in a notorious bandit area.

I climbed stiffly out of the cab grateful to stretch my legs, but soon realised that these checkpoint guards were high on drink and drugs. They looked at the paperwork and started to mime, "Hypodermic needle! Drugs to go in the arm." They were beckoning me to follow them into their wooden guardhouse.

Immediately, I became conscious of my vulnerability. I started to wave my arms making an exaggerated show of anger at their behaviour, whilst quickly making my way back to Paul in Bluebell. The leader followed.

"You no go through. You," pointing at me, "You! Come with me!"

"No way," I was gesticulating. Paul on seeing the danger was ready to move off quickly, and at that very moment three UN vehicles came to the other side of the metal barrier. The barrier was immediately raised for them without question. Quickly scrambling into the cab and ignoring the orders of the drunken guard, I shouted, "Paul, now! Let's go through, now!" Half way through we came alongside the first vehicle.

"OK ahead? Any trouble?" Paul was asking.

"No, It's a nice day, go and enjoy the sunshine!" the driver encouraged in a very casual manner. As the barrier lifted we moved rapidly through making the best of the opportunity afforded us, and sending a quick prayer of thanks 'upstairs.'

Thinking we were now over the last hurdle, we began to relax. I glanced casually into the wing mirror and was shocked to see two cars coming up swiftly behind us. Thankfully we were going downhill! Thankfully we were on tarmac! Thankfully that lone soldier had replaced Bluebell's rubber bush! Thankfully Paul had agreed to re-distribute the load.

I could by this time see four camouflaged, uniformed men in the first car, which had no registration plates. They had rifles. The second car was following close behind. "Paul, whatever you do, don't stop!" No sooner had the words left my mouth than the first car, blowing its horn and flashing its lights, pulled past us on the narrow road and stopped right in front of us. Its doors flew open. Paul somehow held onto the old girl's power steering and miraculously managed to pass between the bandit's open doors and a sheer drop over the edge. He had skilfully squeezed past the hazard, thus avoiding a potentially hideous situation. Again I looked in the wing mirror. The first car was backing up, but the second one was still coming.

Paul drove Bluebell for all he was worth.

"Are they still coming?" he shouted, desperately still trying to control the runaway mare.

"Thank God we are going downhill. Thank God we are on tarmac," I splurged the words

Bluebell was, for eleven years old, absolutely superb. Nothing could touch her. The weight on board was working to our advantage. The old dear couldn't have stopped if we had wanted her to.

The hunters backed off as Bluebell approached a town, which was under control of the pursuers' enemies. We, the hunted, eventually reached relative safety, most grateful to our dear old friend, and the unknown young soldier who replaced the rubber bush.

We arrived at the next UN base quite shaken up, but in our hearts we saw it as a warning to take, if possible, more precautions in future.

The army provided a Warrior Escort, which escorted us through the dreaded pass where the Italians had been murdered. Now this was more than welcome but, to our dismay, we were escorted only a short distance and, for the first time, I was beginning to wish we could afford bullet-proof vests. We realised they gave little protection against the AK47, a weapon that most of the armies used, but they would surely give a sense of protection.

On the next stretch we were all very subdued. I realised what a difference adrenaline pumping through the body makes towards survival. During a crisis, normal functions like hunger and the need to pass water just don't exist. This is an advantage, after all this had been no time to stop and find a bush!

It was clear why the huge professional UN aid lorries drove

like 'bats out of hell,' but for us in Bluebell with such a low undercarriage, the most we could safely do was about 50km per hour. We were grateful to finish the next two-hour stretch unscathed. Even the recently burnt out buildings in Vitez seemed comforting habitation after the bleakness of the journey.

CHAPTER 14

It Was... a Moment in Time

The final run into Zenica brought the usual mixture of emotions, there was trepidation about whether we were actually going to make it, and then hurt as we viewed the local population pulling old carts of wood miles along the single carriageway. In addition there was inner joy at the prospect of seeing the hospital director's face of welcome and recognition for the love and help we wanted to give to all his people. That for me was the actual purpose. Yes, we all had been willing to go back over these monster mountains just to see that smile of appreciation.

This trip was no exception. The director was so amazed and grateful to see the tons of brown boxes being unloaded from Bluebell, that tears were streaming from his tired eyes. He, most of all, knew how much pain and suffering this cargo would save. Looking up with his smiling tear-stained face, he held out both hands.

"Please Jacqui, please tell everybody, please tell everybody in England. Thanks for sending you three."

We each realised we were privileged to be the faces called, on behalf of everybody at home in England, without whom nothing could have been accomplished. To this very day we thank God for everybody who has touched this work and praise Him for every gift that has been given in His name.

The temperature outside must have been in the high thirties but for Paul, lifting heavy boxes inside Bluebell's womb and after such a gruelling week's drive, the physical effort was beyond measure. Every muscle rippled as the sweat ran down his entire body. Jenny's age was no barrier to her contribution to the unloading process. She was a tower of strength, even though shells were exploding, killing people only a few hundred meters away from us, but still Jenny continued working.

As the battle moved closer we all took shelter within the thick walls of the hospital corridor. The solid walls gave comfort, but what we most needed was a shower, something unheard of in this part of the world at this time. Water was measured by the cupful.

The gruelling task eventually finished, we all made our way to the director's office, smelling of excessive perspiration mixed with a covering of earthiness from the red dust. There was a small sink in the office to which we went in turn and sparingly splashed a few drops of water across our foreheads. I dared an extra thimble full under my arms.

Paul was desperately trying to get his hands clean with a small piece of soap, then struggling to wipe the dirt as best he could down the tiny sink. Observing this, the director asked if we would like a shower; but in Bosnia at this time one did not say "yes", because one never knew whose share of anything one might be using. They will always give visitors their best.

Refreshed as well as possible, I sank down into an old well-worn settee wishing my body were not part of me. I ached from top to toe and was aware that my nerves were like tight violin strings.

"That's it Lord I'm spent! I'm sorry, but if you want anything else doing, will you please ask someone else! We are finished! Please can we go home now?"

I should have known better than to say such a thing to my Heavenly Father. What a dreadful thing I had just done in the light of His Holiness.

After saying our emotional farewells we made our way back to the school opposite the flats to park Bluebell for her well earned rest. She seemed to purr as we reached the waiting crowd. Word soon spread and our faithful extended family wasted no time congregating round the back of the old girl.

The vehicle was now empty of aid, apart from a few packets of biscuits which I had held back for the children. Within seconds about fifty people had gathered, mostly women with the children.

In the crowd to my left, I could feel the presence of Ricki taking up his position ready to act as our interpreter by my side. Ricki's tall frame towered above me and the seventeen-year-old young man enjoyed the banter as Paul and Jenny laughed and joked for a while with the crowd to relieve the tension.

Then amongst all the chattering that was going on, my attention was caught by a lady's face, deep in the expectant crowd. Looking at Ricki intently with all her body she seemed to be saying, "Go on! Go on! Ask her!"

For a moment, not sure what was happening, and not speaking a word of the language, I wondered if I was reading her body language correctly. The lady continued urging Ricki,

"Go on! Go on! Ask her!" she seemed to say. With a gift of knowledge I asked.

"Ricki, is that your mother?" I did not give him time to answer. "Is she asking you… to ask us… to take you back to England?"

Ricki bowed his head; a little ashamed anyone would ask such a thing as he knew only too well the dangers for a young man with no papers or passport.

"Ricki do you realise we only have a fifty-fifty chance of

making it back to England? If you are with us we'll have something like… a five percent chance of getting out alive." Now, remembering the horror of the video, I added. "If they catch you, they won't waste bullets on you!"

He stood tall. His gentle countenance seemed to wave in the gentle breeze as he looked down into my eyes. "Jacqui, what difference does it make? It makes no difference. I have no life."

Confused, I desperately panned the sea of anxious faces, searching to find direction as the battle raged within me. My heart urgently wanting to help, but compassion was telling me one thing, my mind telling me another. I could already see the headlines in the newspapers back in England. 'Christians Smuggle!'

My eyes were drawn like a magnet to the mother's face in the crowd; my gaze settled on a small round, tear-stained face, entreating, full of agony and desperation. Ricki's mother pleaded, without words with all her being. A picture of my son, Richard, flashed into my mind.

Moments passed. Moments for both mothers, moments of desperate conflict and inner struggle. By helping Ricki we could be saving his life, or hastening his death. For that moment I would have welcomed a committee to share the responsibility but was glad there wasn't one to prolong the agony.

Again my eyes were drawn, as if irresistibly compelled to the face in the crowd. Finding her gentle presence, our eyes locked, connected, pre-destined. Our mothers' hearts met. Our souls were at one. It was… a moment in time!

Slowly pushing my way through the crowd I reached out and firmly held the lady by her shoulders. Lowering my voice and fighting for the mother's sake to keep my own tears back, I gently yet at the same time, braced myself and said, "We will love him as our own." It was a moment of destiny for both women, a moment of complete surrender.

Quietly I turned to Paul who was in the back of Bluebell starting to unload our personal belongings. My eyes fell on the mattress we had been given by the Irish men on the ferry.

"Paul, bring that mattress, bring your wire cutters," and, looking him straight in the eye, "and PLEASE! PLEASE! Don't ask me any questions why!" This was no time to have a debate.

Turning to Ricki I indicated for him to follow us into the flats. "Please don't say goodbye to your mother now." As naturally as possible we made our way to the flat to figure out how to solve the next problem.

Once safely inside, we set about the difficult task of hollowing out the metal springs to make a space within the mattress. First I asked Ricki to lie diagonally across the mattress on the floor. The mattress was 1.8 metres long. Ricki is almost 2 metres tall. We had to leave at least 10 cms of springs round the edge to help hold the shape.

For hours Paul, Jenny and Edo struggled tirelessly to cut out the thick, metal springs. They took it in turns until their swollen hands bled. The removal of the wadding caused a thick layer of dust that spread right through Nejra's home, yet there was no way she would complain.

The task completed, now was the moment of truth. Ricki crawled under the mattress. He wriggled and squirmed, struggling to fit his large body into the small dark space. At last he was in. "Oh! No! Look at that." There in the middle, undulating with the rhythm of Ricki's heavy breathing, was a big mound. We all looked at it despondently, hearts sinking. "There is nothing else for it," I exclaimed, delighted to have mentally solved the problem, "we will just have to throw all our dirty washing over him and trust the guards will not see the bump! Ricki lie diagonally under the mattress and let's test my theory." It was better.

The next problem was how were we going to get this young man, complete with mattress, into the back of Bluebell without anyone seeing us. "I've got it!" beaming once more. I again had a sense of victory much to everyone else's unease as to what I might come out with next! "We will have to meet Ricki on the motorway after curfew tonight." Now, imagining the darkness I added. "There is no petrol, no lights so there won't be or at least should not be, anyone about."

The tension and apprehension mounted at the mere thought of what I was suggesting. Sensing Paul's unease and disbelief, I challenged, "Well, what else can we do? Has anyone got any better ideas?" There was no response; everyone else only shuffled uneasily. "Then let's do it! Ricki, you go back to your family now and behave normally. Tell no one of the plan. Say goodbye to your mother, father and brother, but understand, you must do it in private. No one must know. We'll all be dead by this time tomorrow, if anyone finds out."

The thought of trying to transport a young man three days' journey through enemy territory, during the height of the war between the Serbs, Muslims and the Croats at this dangerous time, sent shivers down my spine.

Refusing even to think about the consequences, we hurriedly ushered Ricki out of the flat to say his farewells to his family. "Paul, can you imagine what it must feel like for him to have to say goodbye to his family under such dire circumstances." Paul looked past me glassy eyed. I fancied his mind was somewhere else, and this time for once, not on food.

I was so disturbed for the pain which I knew his mother would be experiencing that I took the risk of sitting and writing her a note of comfort, trusting to be able to get someone to deliver it after we had left.

There was only about an hour to wait until curfew, and the whole family including Meho, who by this time had returned from Zagreb, gathered in the flat. Most of them were still shaking their heads in disbelief at the plan.

"What's the problem with Meho?" I asked Zejna. She was reluctant to say. "It's Ricki, isn't it? He is a Muslim and Meho thinks he should be fighting with the rest of his people doesn't he?" I confronted. I knew I had hit the nail on the head.

"Yes, Jacqui. He is not happy on two counts, you are right. He thinks Ricki should go to the front line, but also, he thinks you are taking too much of a risk for him. He doesn't believe you can possibly get him through all those check points. You know they will search you."

Meho and I were very much the same breed, and I understood his sense of responsibility and concern. How could I answer him?

"Zejna, ask Meho what he would have me do if Ricki was HIS son?" Was I looking at double standards? After all hadn't Meho got both his boys out of the country very early on? Zejna interpreted my point. In reply Meho gave me one of those smiles, which says, "Yes – you win! Check Mate!"

Now it was Edo's turn. He spoke about his fears for our safety. "Many people want to kill you Jacqui, they have never met anybody who would do what you are doing. They think you must be making money."

"What! Are you serious Edo? I know you must be, or else you wouldn't say such a wicked thing!" My body was hunched as if I had just received a direct body blow below the belt. Now I could feel the energy of my anger begin to bubble up. It was just as if someone had shaken me like a pop bottle.

"The trouble with these people, whoever they are, 'they' wouldn't do anything without being paid, and they can't understand it when someone else does. I imagine it doesn't matter how many times we come, they will always judge us by their own standards. Well we can live with that," I added now thinking aloud.

"If only they could see. If only we could communicate that we come to share the message of eternal hope through the giving and receiving of forgiveness. After all in John 3 v 16 it says: God so loved the world that he gave His only begotten son, that whosoever believes in Him should not perish but have everlasting life. For God did not send His son into the world to condemn the world, but that the world through Him we might be saved."

"But that's the problem, Jacqui." Paul was now in full flight. "The light has come into the world, and men love darkness. What's changed since the beginning of time? The war in this country, like the wars within ourselves, they come from our own rebellion and guilt feelings and then we want to blame somebody else. Remember it's because of His forgiveness of our sin, that we can even start to love our fellow man. Of course, they don't understand us, Jacqui you should know that!"

I knew Paul was right, but I responded in my usual determined manner. "Well we are not going to respond to fear or intimidation. We're available, so however God wants to use us to show His love for these people through us, He can do it." Paul smiled and hugged me. He loved my childlike determination. He knew I hated all that divides, all which causes us to hurt each other and most of all, I hated it in myself. No wonder 'the enemy' would want to destroy us!

We had to go and collect Ricki. "Jenny, I want you to stay here tonight. There is no point in you being involved in this risky task. After all, if we get caught out after curfew and they put us inside for the night, who will bring us a file to help us escape, if not you?" She understood, bless her. Making little fuss she just wished us well.

The concrete staircase was totally black and even more foreboding than usual. We used the bare minimum of light, making a cover to dim the torch. When we got outside a few refugees were still loitering around Bluebell, taking in the last of the cool night air before retiring into their stuffy overcrowded rooms in the school. As Paul put the key in the ignition Bluebell's engine suddenly sprang into life as if she had been woken from a deep sleep. She was very surprised to be going anywhere at this time of night. "Come on, old girl. It won't be long now. God willing, we will be going home tomorrow then you can have a nice rest."

We drove through the deserted streets. The town was still. A stray dog sniffed the grass, no one had told him about the curfew. The throb of Bluebell's engine seemed to cut through the stillness.

It was only minutes to the motorway and in the dark shadows; we could easily make out Ricki's tall frame silhouetted against the moonlight. Slowly we moved down the slip road and approached him. The humid air was motionless.

This whole area was deserted. It was as if the entire town had suddenly gone down rabbit holes to bed. I remembered the words of my Mother; "Anyone out after 10.30 is up to no good." Maybe not one hundred percent accurate, but I understood the essence of what she was warning me. *'My Lord, she would turn in her grave if she could see us now!'*

Paul switched off the headlights and Bluebell purred to a gentle halt. Only the clicking of crickets interrupted the silence. Wasting no time, Paul jumped out of the cab and briskly moved round to the lorry's back door. I heard the roller shutter go up. In fact the whole of Zenica probably heard the roller shutter door go up as the clatter reverberated round the empty streets.

"Come on Paul!" I was saying under my breath. Bluebell vibrated as Ricki jumped on board. Down came the door again. "Let's get out of here Paul. Stop messing about!" Poor man he could not have done it any quicker if he had tried. Paul threw Bluebell's gears into position and promptly reversed her back up the slip road without using her lights.

"Oh! My Lord If anyone sees this now!" A car came towards us.

"Sausages! Let's see where they go. OK keep going." By this time Bluebell was picking up speed.

"Which way?" Paul was asking. Suddenly everywhere looked unfamiliar. There was not a light anywhere and the moon must have gone behind some clouds. We did not recognise anywhere.

"Paul, I don't know. Don't you know the way?" He made a left turn.

"No! This isn't it. Which way then?" he growled.

"Let's go left again here," I suggested. Dead-end. We were both getting frustrated and started snapping at each other. The tension was clearly taking its toll. "Come on Paul, for goodness sake. It can't be far away. It only took minutes to get here. Where on earth are we?"

"This is it," Paul was saying, "I think this is the other end of the road. Yes, this is the right way." We had taken about twenty minutes for a two-minute journey. Poor Ricki must have thought we had changed our minds about leaving in the morning. Paul carefully manoeuvred Bluebell back into her sleeping place outside the school. Ricki was going to have to remain hidden in her bowels all night. He would not even be able to go to the toilet in the bucket provided in case anyone should hear him.

The light clouds had cleared and the dark sky was jet black. Diamonds twinkled in a heavenly rest. After locking up the cab, Paul came over to where I stood waiting for him on the pavement. Then looking up at the bright Bosnian moon we started strolling back towards the flats.

"Paul, I don't believe we are doing this. I don't believe I'm a housewife from Barnsley and I am doing this! This is the sort of stuff films are made of. Paul, what are we doing?"

He put his arm firmly around my waist as we made our way across the deserted road, pulling me tenderly towards his body for protection.

"Jacqui, you know I don't want to be famous, just effective for God." He paused, speaking with a sense of triumph. "Aren't you glad you're married to me? After all, no one else would be daft enough to do this with you!"

I squeezed his arm, glad that whatever would happen; we were in it together.

In the early hours of the next morning, I rehearsed in my mind the forthcoming scenes of our journey. Daylight brought us the opportunity to at least feel we were able to get on with the job at hand. The packing of our personal things along with the last minute organisation was something with which we had become very familiar. It was done efficiently and quickly. We had hundreds of letters to take back to England, vital links between the refugees and their families. People were always coming to us at the last moment, pressing yet another letter in our hands trusting it would bring the necessary much needed financial help or comfort.

On this occasion however, we needed to slip out of the refugees' lives as smoothly and unobtrusively as possible. The plan was to go to the nearby UN distribution centre and tag on behind the big wagons gaining a sense of security by appearing to belong to the British Convoy. Having been told there was a convoy leaving at 8.30am, we planned to arrive an hour before to give ourselves plenty of time to acquaint the other drivers with Bluebell's limitations.

By 7am having really savoured every mouthful of my final cup of tea with Nejra and the girls, we all shuffled along a narrow passage to the front door and into the darkness and down the twelve flights of concrete stairs. Working hard to keep our conversation normal in the torchlight, we cautiously made our way into the early morning light and further into the unknown of a new day.

As we emerged out of the darkness into the bright, fresh, morning air, Meho and Mujo were waiting nervously, like expectant fathers.

Paul was bringing this now pregnant lady, Bluebell, right alongside us. It took only minutes to load our personal baggage into Bluebell, making sure we threw plenty of dirty washing over the mattress to disguise the tense, pulsating, body beneath.

Little contact with words or movement was made in case we alerted any prying eyes. Meho paced the pavement, clearly disturbed about us leaving, maybe because he had first hand knowledge and experience of the atrocious treatment Ricki, or anyone who helped him, would suffer if we fell into enemy hands.

We didn't know it at the time, but this was the last time we would ever see Meho alive. He was soon to meet a violent death, about which there is still some mystery. It appears that Meho would stop at the checkpoint on the bridge only yards away from his flat in the early hours just a few weeks later. Typically of him, he had decided to go and get the guards some cigarettes from his apartment nearby. That was the last gesture he was to make towards his fellow countryman.

Five days later he was found at the bottom of the lift shaft after falling or being pushed from the seventh floor. There were burn marks down his legs where he tried to save himself clinging onto the metal rope in a desperate last attempt to survive.

CHAPTER 15

The Great Escape

Only yards from Meho's future concrete tomb, Nejra and the girls were doing their best to be cheerful, but it was obvious this lovely lady was having great difficulty in controlling her emotions. Edo bowed and shook his head, almost unable to accept we might never get through again. After all, we had become their and the refugees' only link with the outside world. Losing connection with us would leave Edo and his family feeling more helpless and destitute than ever. We all experienced the bond of love between us ripping away at our hearts, as we prepared for what could be the final goodbye.

'*How Ricki's family must be suffering at this time,*' I thought, '*and Ricki, in the darkness of Bluebell's womb, will need to muster every bit of courage to stay put.*' Quickly I pushed those thoughts aside. '*Come on Paul, let's get out of here*'.

Cracking my imaginary whip, John Wayne style, I shouted, "Wagons Ho! Let's roll." For a moment there were smiles and feeble waves as Bluebell slowly but firmly pulled away for the start of the long difficult labour which would have to be endured if there was ever to be a birth into freedom.

The sun was already high in the sky as we arrived at the UN base. Pulling in behind some Land Rover type vehicles I was pleased to see the familiar, black smiling face of the convoy leader.

"How are you doing? What time are you leaving?" I asked.

"Probably about 11.30."

"11.30! What happened to 8.30?"

"There's been some trouble ahead, and we're hanging on a bit until we get confirmation we can proceed."

Already feeling the heat of the day and realising the temperature would be well into the eighties by mid-morning; I looked up at the clear blue sky, shook my head and slowly walked back towards the cab.

"Paul, it looks like we're going to have something like a three-hour wait. Can you, in a minute, go to the back and very quietly communicate to Ricki? You'll have to go in and pull the roller shutter door down after you so no one sees the activity. Before you do Paul, let's just pull over to that spot over there, it's a bit quieter."

I pointed to an eight-foot high wire fence situated near the beginning of the convoy. "If we wait there, then when the convoy pulls out, we'll be well positioned to tag on without too much trouble."

Paul rolled the old lady into position. As soon as we had parked, Jenny immediately tried to jump out of the cab.

"No Jenny! Stay here with me and let Paul deal with it," I requested firmly.

"But I could be getting something out of my bags!" she protested.

"No Jenny! We're all experiencing a lot of tension and we need to calm ourselves a lot more or else they'll wonder what's up. I know you are worried about Ricki but I think you'll have difficulty in behaving naturally. I know you want to give him support, which I understand, but we are already very conspicuous." Jenny tried to protest again. I cut her short, spelling out the obvious.

"Do you realise Jenny, we are the only blue lorry in the compound and the only one with two females on board. These men have nothing better to do than to glue their eyes on Bluebell and our sylph like figures"

Jenny stayed where she was, quite frustrated but willing to concede and whilst we waited, we amused ourselves by watching the soldiers throwing a few apples to the children gathered at the fence. They seemed to be cheerful little souls, at least until the apples landed the other side of the fence. Then they became tyrants, the bigger ones exerting their strength over the younger ones to grab all the goodies for their own use.

The nearer the time moved to the 11.30 departure time, the greater the anxiety of our trio.

"Paul, when this convoy starts off, whatever you do keep well up to them! Don't leave any spaces because you know in this first section there are a lot of refugees waiting outside those gates and if we get separated at the beginning we'll never be able to catch up!"

One Warrior led the convoy, followed by nine, sixteen-tonne giant lorries. Pregnant Bluebell brought up the rear. Paul wasted no time in leaving the compound. The sun was hot and we were grateful to feel some air blowing through the cab.

Paul and I were both on high alert. One wrong move could jeopardise our chances of getting through the checkpoint between the end of the motorway and the beginning of the mountains about six miles further on.

"Paul, it looks as if they'll drive straight through this checkpoint. Come on! Keep closer then we'll get through with them!" By this time we were well into our top speed for the conditions, hugging the bends as best we could.

Jenny and I were hanging on to Bluebell's sides like warbles, flies under the skin of a horse. Bluebell was clearly enjoying herself. She was like a young mare released from her cramped stable. Paul rode uncompromisingly round every bend and Bluebell bounced over every bump.

"Paul, we'll never make it at this rate! If she hits any of those boulders, we'll be finished!"

"Jacqui, Shut up! I'm not losing them now." Bluebell was now like a thoroughbred pulling at the bit. Paul used his gear stick as a whip to encourage her to go faster. She tried her best to work with him, but clouds of dust from the vehicles in front blew up like a dense fog which was blinding us. Paul and Bluebell were running with blinkers on.

"Back off Paul. You must back off! She can never keep this pace up for six hours!"

Actually I could have saved my breath because the further we climbed up the mountains, the more the convoy pulled out of sight, until it became only a cloud of dust somewhere in the distance.

We were again trundling along on our own at a mere trot instead of a gallop. There was solid rock to our left, a sheer drop to a river on our right with a dense wood spreading into a green backdrop.

We were all beginning to feel a little more comfortable as the sun was now shining and the visibility had improved considerably, when all of a sudden, we heard a sharp hiss, quickly followed by a blue flash darting across the front of the windscreen.

"Sniper fire! Sniper fire!" I shouted. "Drive! Drive! Drive!" We heard the second bullet hit the top of Bluebell and, in a sudden silence as if in slow motion, the window on Paul's side shattered into a million pieces.

"Get down Jacqu!." Paul was shouting at me. "Get down!"

"Get down Jenny!" We were all shouting simultaneously.

Down on my haunches, my head just appearing over the

bottom of the windscreen, I was shouting directions for all I was worth.

"Right! Left! Paul, Right! Right! Drive! Drive, Drive! Keep driving!" Paul, anticipating death, expecting the next bullet to be his, was driving with his head and torso flat down over the steering wheel.

"Lord, don't let us die here! Lord! Don't let us die in this dirt!" I continued to pray out loud, now in tongues, the words tumbled from my lips. Words I had not heard before. The sound of machine gunfire continued, 'Tat – tat – tat.'

Totally immobilised by fear all I could do was to think, '*if Paul gets shot now I won't have the courage to move across into the driver's seat!*' I could see the scene in the film where the co-driver on the stagecoach gets hold of the reins and saves the day. At that moment I knew I lacked the bottom line courage.

"Keep going Paul, please keep going!"

Our lives depended on Paul keeping his nerve and driving fiercely forward. Bluebell was being whipped and lashed for all she was worth!

Without moving I visualised myself cowering in the corner on the cab floor waiting helplessly for our assailants to come and cut our throats. 'Tat – Tat – Tat- Tat!'

"I don't believe… it's still coming!" The continuous sound that echoed through the valley, felt like there was no getting away from the demons of hell. I had always imagined sniper fire to be one single, deliberate, shot from a lone figure looking through a telescopic lens, not fifty continuous rounds.

To my relief, Paul was still driving, still with his head and torso flat across the steering wheel. We turned another bend and, apart from the roar of Bluebell's engine and the pounding of our heartbeats, there was an unreal silence, but we still hurtled along at top speed in case more snipers were waiting around the next bend.

I glanced across at Paul; blood was trickling down the side of his face and running into the hairs on his chest. There was no doubting the courage of this man who had just saved all our lives!

Taking a deep breath both Jenny and I struggled apprehensively, and very tentatively, back up on to the seats. As soon as we had recovered our composure, Jenny pointed to the scorch marks of a bullet hole in the doorframe on the near side of Bluebell, only millimetres from a picture of Jesus.

"That bullet must have come through your side of the window Paul, across in front of our chests and straight through the opposite doorframe on Jenny's side." Stunned into silence, we were all unable to take in the reality we had just experienced. We had just narrowly escaped death.

Within a matter of yards we came to the end of this treacherous section of the route. This was the exact place where the Italians had been killed. There, by the grace of God, we had made it! We realised it must have been by the flutter of an angel's wing. We were all quite unable to take it in.

Now, seemingly enjoying the scenery sat one British UN Warrior! Two soldiers perched out of the top of the turret complete with guns in hand. Slowly because she was still in shock and wounded, Bluebell limped by in front of the large dusty tank. Paul pushed his elbow straight through the remaining shattered glass on his side window and shouted quite deliberately. "Where the b---dy h—— were you when we needed you?" My usually mild, kind husband clearly was not amused.

Already my mind was racing ahead. *'What if Ricki is dead in the back? Shall we turn right and go to the base? What should we do if we have a dead body on board? Should we just go to the UN and say, excuse me we have a dead Muslim on board, what shall we do next?'*

I looked ahead; "There's the dust of the convoy ahead. Look we can just see them. We're on tarmac for these few miles; let's see if we can catch them up before the next mountain road."

Realising that the bullet holes and the smashed window might draw unwanted attention to our vehicle, I changed my instruction. "No, slow down Paul! Let's drive through here as if all is fine!"

"What about Ricki?" Jenny was asking.

The truth was, I dare not let my mind even address this question let alone answer it, but I knew I would have to eventually.

"I'm sorry Jenny, he's either dead or alive but, we definitely can't stop to check now we are still in bandit country. What time is it?"

"It's a quarter to twelve," Paul replied. Looking across at him, I was grateful to see his wounds were only superficial.

"It's a quarter to twelve on a Monday morning," I continued, still trying to get hold of the situation. "Goodness, Jenny, what are we normally doing at a quarter to twelve on a Monday morning? I'll tell you this, if we get out of this little lot, then I'll be happy to do just the washing on a Monday morning for the rest of my life."

Jenny quite understandably was still worrying about Ricki. "Jenny, we'll stop as soon as we dare, but for the moment we are going to have to trust that God has looked after Ricki."

I allowed my mind just a little space to imagine what it must have been like for him in Bluebell. "Can you imagine being in the dark under that mattress, on bare wood, with those metal springs sticking in your flesh and hearing all that machine gun fire? Can you imagine what it must have been like being tossed over all those bumps at top speed? How could he have survived?" My heart sank…but I was still unwilling to face the possibilities that we may have killed him.

We journeyed on, still in shock, still unable to absorb the reality of our escape but still desperately trying to gain some composure.

"When you think of it, when you think we were probably travelling forward at some considerable speed when that bullet came sideways across our chests, then you realise God must have had an angel deflecting those bullets!"

These thoughts were still racing around in my head when Bluebell was halted, at the beginning of the next mountain pass, by a line of stationary vehicles. It appeared one of the lorries of the original convoy had blown a tyre, and nobody could get past.

Jenny was quite taken with a bright yellow lorry parked to our left. A lady standing by a vehicle bearing the words, 'Edinburgh Direct Aid' smiled a big warm open smile and waved in acknowledgement of fellow citizens. "A British lorry. Thank God for them. Let's pray they have an easier time going through that stretch than we did." Jenny waved, and again the warmth of that lady's smile seemed to move in empathy towards our trembling hearts.

We were able to move up a few yards and halted practically alongside Martin Bell, the BBC news reporter who was inside an armoured Land Rover travelling in the opposite direction.

Trying to block out our frightening experience with light-hearted banter, we chatted with the crew about everything except our deadly secret.

One of the crew members was kindness itself and offered us a couple of oranges and an apple. Unobtrusively I went round to the back of Bluebell, and lifted the roller shutter door enough to allow space to roll the fruit along the floor, trusting it would refresh Ricki, should he still be alive!

Martin Bell stomped around and complained to Paul how annoyed he was to be held up. I kept quiet wanting to say how lucky he was, able to travel in his bullet proof Land Rover. I was glad that was all he had to complain about. Instead, I pondered in my heart on how very close Mr. Bell was to a headline story, but kept quiet, also knowing we were not out of trouble yet. When at last we were able to move forward, within a few minutes the convoy in front was well out of sight, we trundled on bringing up the rear.

"If we keep going we will soon be able to find a quiet place to stop," Paul said breaking into my thoughts. I was still blocking what I did not want to know about Ricki's condition.

Within about half an hour we came across a small group of French Canadian troops 'dug in' at a rather large clearing at the side of the road.

"Stop here, Paul, let's see what's what." Paul took little persuading.

As soon as he jumped out of Bluebell, the soldiers, seeing blood on his head and down his front, quickly carted him off to their small first aid post. Jenny wasted no time in getting out and searching unsuccessfully for a toilet. The soldiers, with great amusement, offered her a bedpan and politely turned their backs whilst she used it.

A big burly Sergeant strode over to the driver's side of the cab. On seeing me, who must have looked less than my usual manicured self, roared in a jovial voice, hands on hips, "And now lady, what can I do for you?" I hesitated momentarily, then without hesitation, dropped from the height of the cab above, straight into his strong, long arms.

"Please give me a hug?" He held me tightly and for a moment, I felt secure and safe.

"Thank you. I needed that!" Then, professional till the last, and as an after thought, I added "Oh! Incidentally, have you got any diesel?"

Jenny, having used the bedpan in the back of the army truck, joined me standing alongside Bluebell's petrol tank. Simultaneously we looked down, our eyes drawn to a large bullet hole exactly where the mattress would have been positioned. Stomachs churning, heads motionless, our eyes fell to the ground. Was there any blood dripping through the floorboards? It was essential we acted as normally as possible. We couldn't admit to ourselves that Ricki was either dead or injured. Was there anything we could do or say to help him at that moment without inhibiting his chances of getting out?

I was relieved the tense atmosphere was broken when Paul returned quite happy after receiving the professional care of the soldiers who had removed fragments of glass from his scalp, whilst other soldiers took a video of this strange blue vehicle sporting a new type of ventilation.

Desperately needing to find a place where we could be on our own to check on Ricki's situation, we had to drive along for about ten further minutes before feeling secure enough to pull over behind some giant rocks away from prying eyes.

Now was the time to face the truth. I stayed in the cab, unwilling to face the possibility I could have been responsible for killing Ricki. Paul and Jenny walked swiftly around to the back of Bluebell.

I sat there, too scared to go and look, motionless, every sense alert. The roller shutter door went up.

"Ricki! Are you there?" No response.

"Ricki! Ricki! Are you there?" Paul's voice was getting more urgent. A loud "Alleluia" rang out from the back of the vehicle.

Ricki must have responded! I could scarcely contain my delight. Praises were swelling up to Heaven. Hearts were overflowing with praise and thanksgiving.

"What a Mighty Father we have. Alleluia! Alleluia! And Lord! Would you mind if Bluebell becomes Saint Bluebell from now on?"

It took many more hours to travel over the rest of the mountains. We were aware we had peace in our hearts knowing that, despite one of the bullets coming within millimetres of Ricki's head, another passing through St. Bluebell's side and coming out just behind our backs, we undoubtedly had been protected by the grace of God.

If we had been protected this far we felt much more confident about the rest of the journey. At least we felt confident until we came to the border checkpoint between Bosnia and Croatia.

Stopping to show the papers, our eyes moved apprehensively along a line of armed men standing in true 'Rambo' style.

"These papers, no good!" I reached for the next layer.

"We go back to England. Empty." 'Rambo' looked again then beckoned to Paul.

"Open. Open!" he ordered. My heart sank, and pleading inside I cried out.

'Not now. They can't find him now!'

"Open!" 'Rambo' repeated pointing to the back of St. Bluebell.

Paul slowly, reluctantly, taking as long as he possibly could, dismounted from the cab. It took him exactly five paces to reach the back of St. Bluebell. Watching in the wing mirror I counted every step.

"One…two…three…four…five!" Six men, complete with machine guns, moved with him around to the back of St. Bluebell out of sight.

"Pray in tongues, Jenny!" I encouraged. This could be the last time I see my husband alive I thought.

I am sure Jenny was praying for all she was worth. I was sure we were all hardly able to contemplate the next few moments. The roller shutter door went up, slowly. I felt the whole of St. Bluebell bounce as the guards jumped inside.

One, two, three we could feel the vibrations! They must now be standing right next to the mattress. '*Lord... Put a hedge around that boy! Blind their eyes! In fact do whatever you have to do, but Lord please do it now!*' Helplessly I threw my hands in the air. I hoped the washing still covered the bump.

Silence...those moments became a lifetime. Then the sound of the door closing. It reverberated like a drum roll bringing down the final curtain at the end of an ugly movie. Jenny and I waited.

In the wing mirror I could see Paul swaggering back, hardly able to restrain the smile from bursting through on to his ashen face. He entered the cab.

"I don't believe it. They actually kicked the mattress and saw nothing!" We couldn't believe it either. It seemed incredible that we could have had another such narrow escape.

We were relieved when we realised that we were only a short distance from a house where we had rested on previous journeys. We wasted no time in heading there! This home was right in the middle of a town and had always been safe for us. However, now we had a shot up lorry, and although it made no difference to us given our impartiality, we were carrying a Muslim in Croat territory, so would it still be safe?

By the time we arrived I had already worked out a master plan.

"Wait here you guys. Let me go and see if I can get some help." The household was surprised to see my tall silhouette through their glass door. Welcoming me enabled the family to release the tension and quell the anxiety they had been feeling about us all since we last met.

"If it's all right with you, please can we stay and rest here a while with a friend? We need to get him out of St. Bluebell and into the house." My mind was already actively engaged in the logistics.

I mustered up five assorted sized males. "Come on boys, I've got a job for you. Come on, Paul! Let's get you men inside St. Bluebell to help unload our bags."

Paul said nothing, and I was sure that he couldn't understand my logic. Five men boarded St. Bluebell and six emerged into the bright sunlight, heading straight for the safe house.

The signs of strain on Ricki's face were beyond imagination. He had been in the back of St. Bluebell for twenty-two hours. What it must have been like for him being bounced on bare floor boards, alone in the dark, under that dusty mattress with sharp metal spikes sticking into him, through twenty odd check points was beyond my imagination. He had not dared to breathe when the guards had entered the lorry not knowing if the next breath would be his last.

Once inside we hugged each other in some sort of disbelief, and it took some time before we even began to relax. The mother of the house quickly produced a clean, white t-shirt to replace Ricki's dusty, sweaty one. He was offered a warm shower and needed little persuasion to enjoy what must have been one of the biggest gifts anyone could have given him at that time. This was the love of God in operation. Not Croats or Muslims, but decent human beings.

I imagined Eternity and wondered how God would re-pay our host's kindness. Surely He would give these people a crown of honour; surely they were princes amongst princes.

Refreshed, and unwilling to put the family at any more unnecessary risk, we were keen to get Ricki safely back on board. This was achieved by merely reversing the original strategy, six boarded, five emerged.

The next part of the run to the ferry should only have taken two to three hours but it was now late in the day. Paul was deeply concerned about us being on the road after dark and especially in our shot up state.

We would have to take a chance and ask to stay at another house we knew, but would Zdravko a Croat, give sanctuary to Ricki and St. Bluebell? There would be a welcome for the Brits but I was not so sure about Ricki, a Muslim, or St. Bluebell in her damaged state. There was nothing for it, we would have to risk it as the ferry was not due to depart for another seventeen hours, and we certainly couldn't be on the streets for that length of time.

Very wearily and quite reluctantly, we headed towards what we hoped would be an 'oasis in the middle of the desert.' I thought of the scripture. 'When you receive one of mine, you receive me' for I knew this particular family had hearts of gold but could they find it in their hearts to receive a Muslim?

When we arrived at the house I decided to test the ground. "Wait here. Let me go in first and explain the situation. We must not compromise these people. They must freely make their choice."

Before I reached the door the children had spotted the holes in the vehicle.

"Come and see this!" they called to their father. The sight of a bullet ridden lorry in any of our front gardens would cause some curiosity!

"Mama Mia! Oh! My God! Oh! My God!"

By this time Zdravko's hands were way up in the air. "Oh! My God! What has happened to you?"

"Zdravko, we need your help. We need to park the lorry here over night, but we do not want to put your family at risk."

"Come in. Come in. You people my friends."

"Wait," I was saying, holding him by the arm. "You don't know the whole picture yet. Let me explain before you make your decision."

It is fair to say Zdravko was rightly very apprehensive when he learnt of Ricki's presence in the back of St. Bluebell. He needed time to consider, and withheld his decision until after refreshment. Having eaten and drunk plenty he suddenly commanded, "Fetch the boy. He sleeps upstairs." Decision made. We could all stay.

Paul went to fetch Ricki. Jenny and I witnessed the beautiful way in which his oldest daughter sweetly and lovingly tuned into Ricki's situation. Her heart was reaching out to him in total compassion. 'A child shall lead them.' One could see she was imagining what he must have been through.

It was not the easiest of nights. Paul and I were thankful to be offered the bed settee facing the front door. I watched that door most of the night, worried in case our dear host had a change of heart and went to phone the authorities from the phone box at the corner of his lane. I need not have worried. To this day the whole family have been most faithful, and I could see why our Heavenly Father had led us to this home on that first occasion. God is the master player in the game of chess, and we thankfully are His pieces.

Thinking about the journey ahead, I realised we still had a long way to travel and I was continually mentally working though the logistics of the forthcoming ferry journey. I could see many potential dangers, and we all spent much time in prayer before surrendering the situation unto His care.

By the following day we had to wait before boarding the ferry in Split and stress levels were again greatly heightened. Finally the staff of the ferry company were ready to load, and we watched as they instructed everyone where to position the vehicles on board. The heat in the bowels of the ship was tremendous and hit us like a tidal wave, and this was even before the main steel loading doors were closed.

No sooner had we parked and the chains positioned round our wheels when we saw a lorry pull up only inches behind St. Bluebell's rear door. This would prevent any means of escape into fresh air. *'Ricki can't possibly survive the night in this heat and breathing in these fumes'*, I mused, *'there's no fresh air whatsoever.'* No sooner had the thought entered my head, then in a moment of panic, I shouted.

"Stop! Stop! I need my toothbrush out of the back."

"Yes!" Jenny agreed, "I need my bag as well." Bless her; just waking up to the fact that she really did need it. Between us we created such a commotion, the poor staff working to get the last vehicle on board behind us signalled for the lorry parked directly behind us to move back a few feet.

"What on earth are you two girls doing?" Paul was getting annoyed. "What are you messing about at?"

"Paul, we need our bags for the night. We must be able to get into the back of St. Bluebell. One cannot breathe down here!" I was hoping he was reading my double meaning. Dutifully he opened up the old girl's back door. First lowering the hydraulic ramp, and then slowly pushing up the roller door just enough to enable him to get inside and get out our bags. I stood watching and praying.

"What now Lord? What are we going to do?" To my absolute amazement the lorry behind us didn't bother to close the gap, and there was some space for later manoeuvres when all was quiet.

We could do nothing more for the time being so made our way up to our cabin, one small three berth. There was not enough room to swing a cat and the heat was overpowering. We fiddled with the air conditioning, but it made no difference. This was not going to be a comfortable night.

To kill time and relieve some of the tension we went for a meal and hoped no one would guess our secret. Jenny began talking to an aid worker returning home to England who seemed to want to attach himself to us.

"Get Jenny away from that man," I was instructing Paul, unable to deal with the situation calmly myself. I was worried Jenny, in her generosity of spirit would give the game away.

"Let's just all go back into the cabin," thinking we wouldn't make any mistakes there. I was probably the one who would make the mistakes now as my nerves had completely gone. I was only just hanging in there.

Once inside the comparative safety of the cabin, I put an Alan Pimlot tape on my little recorder. Paul and I had shared many peaceful and joy filled hours worshipping with this anointed singer. The gentle sound of his melodic voice brought the calm we needed. We rested, prayed and worshipped, enjoying as best we could the less than perfect situation.

"Paul, its 10.30. That boy's been down there five hours. He must be nearly suffocating by now. We can't leave him down there any longer."

"Jacqui, we can't risk bringing him up."

"Paul, we will have to. Will you please go down and see if you can get him up here?"

"I'll go too," Jenny said, excited at the prospect of seeing Ricki again.

"No, Jenny, you stay here. Paul will be better off on his own." Jenny was clearly hurt, but willing to accept, that none of us had the strength to argue.

Jenny made the best of the time by joining me in prayer for a covering, from the immediate dangers. Maybe only seven or eight minutes later there was a quiet tap on the door. We held our breath. It was Paul and Ricki. "Praise God! We were so grateful as for now, all was well!"

After our initial relief that Ricki was with us, we all tried to sleep, a near impossibility in the stifling heat. Four bodies in such a small space made it difficult for us to rest and we gained no relief for our physical tiredness. Jenny tried waving the door back and forth to create some movement of air. It helped a little. When she finally settled down, I found myself keeping door watch. I tried to sleep with one eye and two ears open, and comforted myself with the thought that Ricki was at least with us and not still in St. Bluebell's burning womb.

By 6am we were still as tired as we were when we first lay down. Paul escorted Ricki back down into the bowels of the ship. Jenny and I kept a prayer covering over the situation, and were relieved when Paul returned, mission safely accomplished.

The usual hustle and bustle started as lorry drivers and families returned to their vehicles ready to disembark. As the doors of the ferry opened up, everyone was relieved to be getting their first taste of fresh air for twelve hours. St. Bluebell rolled out, a bit like Jonah coming out of the mouth of a giant whale.

After what we'd been through getting out of Bosnia, the Croatian, Slovenian and Austrian border crossings were all taken in our stride. Our main problem now would be on arrival in England.

How were we going to get Ricki into England? Were we going

to declare him? Would the authorities send him back? I wrestled with all these worries throughout the whole of Germany and Belgium. So I decided to write a full statement to have ready for whatever situation came up. Not wishing in my heart to deceive anyone or to flout the law of the land, I wished to be open as to how our Heavenly Father had moved the chess pieces in this situation.

In case we became separated when we arrived on British soil, we made sure Ricki had, in his possession, money, various phone numbers and our addresses. Days later following the lorry in front we passed through customs and on to passport control with three passports ready at hand.

However, when replacing the shattered glass, Zdravko, bless him, had completely sealed the driver's window. This meant Paul had to open St. Bluebell's door to show the passports, which slowed down the queue. To save time the officer in charge waved Paul straight through.

We could not believe our luck! What were we actually experiencing? I soon became conscious of the speed ramps and remembered we had passed over them on our way into the docks.

"Well, if we passed over them on the way in, then we must, by now, be well on our way out! We're through! We're in England. Lord, we've made it!" My hand punched the air. Excitement welled up, so elated were we; the cab was too small to hold our explosion of exhilaration and thanksgiving.

"Come on you guys. It's four o'clock on a Saturday afternoon. The sun is shining. Let's park Bluebell and show Ricki the ferry he has just come off!"

Overflowing with thankfulness just to be alive, all four of us were like spring lambs skipping with light hearts, arm-in-arm along the cliff path as we surveyed the beautiful shimmering sea, which separated our treasured little island from the vastness of Europe. It was a moment to savour. I remembered my school song, 'This Royal throne of Kings, this Sceptre Isle, This earth of Majesty, This Seat of Mars…This precious stone set in the silver sea. This Earth. This Realm. This England.'

Although it would take another five hours to reach home, nothing could dampen our high spirits. The journey up the motorway seemed to last forever. We were about to discover how powerfully God had moved in Ricki's life, how many similarities there were to Joseph in the Old Testament times.

Here was a young man who had been plucked from his mother's arms and transported by complete strangers across the other side of the continent. Here was Jenny sharing with him Joseph's story so he could get just a glimpse of how much God was in his situation. Ricki told how he used to live with his close-knit family in a five-bedroom house, set in five hectares of ground.

Then, simply because they were Muslims, life changed horrifically over night. First his father and mother were both sacked from their jobs. Suddenly their world went crazy as their fellow neighbours and school friends started a systematic 'cleansing process' of all Muslims from the area. For two weeks they slept in the woods which surrounded their home. Other neighbours were setting homes alight. Their world went crazy and nothing made any sense any more. The situation of war meant someone from his class at school would quite happily shoot him. Not for who he was, but for what he was.

There was no one to turn to, no one to tell 'them' to stop. Then the family had to sign a paper saying it was not their home any more. If they did not sign they were to be shot. Eventually hundreds of Muslims were herded together like animals on to cattle wagons and taken to a camp, but not before 'they' opened fire and killed some of their fellow neighbours, one being Ricki's school friend. The family had looked on horrified. There was nothing they could do, they were helpless.

In the camp they slept on the floor, all four were surviving on one small tin of beans between them. Ricki and his brother were lucky; they found some manual work for nine hours a day which gave them enough money to supplement the family diet to buy one piece of bread a day. Ricki told us that, despite the lack of sanitation, electricity or running water, he would have stayed with his family had it not been for the fact that all the young men were rounded up and sent to the Bosnian armies front line; to be used as 'cannon fodder.' He would have been expected to kill his own people or be killed. It was then that he knew he would risk death to escape. Somehow they had missed him in the original round up, but he was due to go into the army in five days time, so literally he would have been sent to die, fighting for the people who took everything from them. He said, "At least that is what would have happened, if you guys had not come along. The worst bit for me was when I was cowering inside the cramped mattress, parked outside the school, when I heard my mother's voice. It was then I cried, but I cried quietly."

'We guys' sat in stunned silence, trying to grasp the enormity of what God had done with our simple faith and obedience. We travelled on in silence, each lost in our own thoughts.

Eventually, Jenny, complete with all her worldly goods, was safely returned into the welcome embrace of her closest available family member, Marco Polo, her dear old cat. He rubbed his firm, furry body along her gamely, ageing frame. They were together again.

Paul and I still had a few more miles to travel before our reunions. Radiant with happiness, glowing with joy, yet with no real comprehension of what God had done through us, we turned the last corner into our own road.

The yellow streetlights and warmth from friendly homes welcomed us into the bosom of our estate family. We drew up slowly, St Bluebell's engine purred almost regally outside our own front door. The lights of home shone, welcoming us back into a safe harbour.

As St. Bluebell's engine gave her final, gentle groan, Ruza emerged from our home. Her arms opened wide. Warmth, love and comfort poured out through every pore of this lady from Bosnia. We could hardly contain our excitement, amongst the entire bustle of greetings, hugging and kissing. Ricki crossed the threshold into a safe family home. Excited chatter bubbled as we enjoyed a welcome cup of tea.

"Come on Ricki, you can sleep in Richard's big double bed tonight. You can really stretch out and even watch television if you want."

Leaving him to adjust to his new surroundings, I filled a bath with pure, clear, hot water before releasing oils to create a sea of perfumed froth.

"Ricki, have a bath," I invited, handing him a large warm towel. "When you've finished jump into bed and I will bring you a lovely mug of hot chocolate."

It wasn't long before this young man was sitting up wrapped in the warmth and comfort of a cosy, soft duvet. I sat on the edge of the bed, leaned back against the fresh, cotton pillow and put my arm around his broad shoulders. He responded instinctively by gently resting his weary head against me. I tenderly, lovingly stroked his forehead and kissed his thick, black hair,

"You're safe! You're home! Sleep well! Good Night! God Bless! Now we must look to God for your family!"

CHAPTER 16

News at Ten

It wasn't long after we returned home with Ricki before the bullet holes in Saint Bluebell were being noticed. We realised a decision would have to be made regarding the declaration and legalisation of him. Further I needed to test what my own instincts were telling me, so I took counsel from a minister friend a few miles away.

"Well I know what I would do," the friend said.

"Tell me," I encouraged, believing what he was about to advise would tie up exactly with my own thoughts.

"Simply declare it the way it happened and do it now!"

Delighted his advice merely confirmed my own thoughts and not worrying about the consequences, my next concern was how exactly to go about it?

Immediately after the receiver was replaced, the phone rang.

"This is Caroline Kerr, from *News at Ten*. We are doing a programme about people from Bosnia in this country. Do you mind if we interview you about the situation out there?" I was quite used to my Heavenly Father working fast.

'But Lord, is this the way you really want it? Do you really want this to hit the headlines?' Before I could gather my thoughts there I was verbally reliving the whole story.

From that moment on, for the next few days our home resembled Piccadilly Circus. Within an hour there were television cameras and wires everywhere. At one time there was a television crew in the lounge, another in the kitchen and our garden playing host to yet a third. Ricki remained calm and composed in the middle of these entire proceedings. After all, we could do nothing other than tell the truth and trust we would come out of this situation as safely as possible.

Much to our embarrassment, the headlines appeared as 'The Great Escape.' We were all heralded (however reluctantly) as heroes. At no time then or now did we ever believe ourselves to be brave. Deep down we all knew, without any shadow of doubt, our own nothingness in the situation. Each one of us had known the moment of naked danger, real terror. We had looked death squarely in the face and we could all remember the moments of fear and dread when the bullets came. We could each still feel and re-experience in every quiet moment, a gripping all consuming fear which confirmed for each of us over and over again, we were anything but brave!

With nerves still raw I recorded how it felt at the time.

"There is a sense of being on hold. Not being able to start life again.

Waiting…waiting for what? Permission to start to live again?
Can we give ourselves that permission?

There seems to be no relief, a sense of unreality prevails.
The world is moving fast yet we are on hold…unable to get back in touch with living.

We need space to recharge…we are not able to recharge because we are holding the responsibility, and it's awesome. It's as if our eyes are on the job, which still needs to be completed…yet we are held… suspended.

We have life, but…don't seem to be able to give ourselves permission to live it.

What should we do? Wait? No. Paul, needs help... he is suffering.
I feel his pain...I hear it... behind the jokes and the smiles when he
closes his eyes... the dreams, the screams.
We must break the cycle. We must get back in touch with reality.
We trust the fear will lessen. Will it subside?
We must allow time to become the welcome healer.
We know inside, there is no escape.
We know inside...we must go back...we must continue.
The risks are great and we know there could be persecution.
Everyone will view what we have done differently.
In Bosnia it will be viewed one way...in Croatia another...
the authorities will view it another...the Church will see it yet another.
We feel alone. So what next? The nightmares will have to continue.
We know they will subside.
The dreams for us are worse than reality, but not so for the people of
Bosnia.
Their reality is worse than any of our dreams.
jr

Ricki was also burdened. He was holding the fear inside,
carrying the horror for his family and his people. They were still
in the living hell. Then graciously and lovingly like a precious gem,
God cast a healing gift into his morass of uncertainty and pain.

The *News at Ten* films were sold on the world network and
shown in Zagreb. The transmission was immediately picked up by
an amateur radio ham, who promptly radioed the news into
central Bosnia. Within three weeks of Ricki leaving Bosnia, his
family, by the grace of God, had heard that he had made it to
England. They knew he was alive, safe and well. For Ricki this was
yet another unbelievable gift.

By the end of 1993, we lived daily with the worsening situation
in Bosnia. Besides the continuing attempt of all the attacking

forces to take and re-take land, whilst at the same time cleansing the Balkans of as many civilian males as possible, the Croats and the Muslim, were now fighting each other. Guerrilla warfare was waged over every pocket of land and every village. The savage enemy was doing its worst, claiming the title deeds of each heart and home with each penetrating assault.

This may have been a simplistic way of looking at the conflict, but the way I saw it; three different sides were now fighting for the same territory. One side fought for power, one for perceived rights, and the third for sheer survival. Our allegiance was equal to all ethnic groups at an individual level.

However not all traffic was one way, because by March 1996 Ruza had decided to return to her former home in a town called Ilijas, situated within a half-hour drive from Sarajevo. By this time the town had just been liberated by the Bosnian army and held under the Dayton agreement. Neither Paul nor I were happy with her decision to return, as by this time she was very comfortably situated in her own home five minutes away from us. Whilst we understood her reasons to be part of the re-building process, we had grave concerns about her well being. The only thing which gave us some comfort, was the fact that she had measured well the interpretation of some Islamic extremists and Christianity and had come to the conclusion in her own mind to open her heart recognising her need of a Saviour.

The whole experience had happened unbeknown to us in the back of a taxi one evening in Bradford. She had gone to the bus station to meet her two nephews who had been in hiding at her brother's home in Croatia. We had met them in the early part of the war.

On hearing that the two young men were from Bosnia the taxi driver assumed that they must be Muslims. He then went on to describe the very calculating way in which he and others intended to infiltrate our 'Christian' society in England with the express desire to finally see the law of our country changed in favour of their cultural and religious preferences. Quite simply, Ruza measured the motives of his heart against what she had found were the motives of our hearts, and firmly decided to stand one side of the religious divide. She wanted and was indeed now ready to invite Jesus Christ into her own life. The following Sunday, she asked to come to our church and once there, she made a public confession of her faith.

Mirza, Ruza's eldest son, was still in America having just graduated from Wittenberg University. Deni her youngest son, the original boy at the fence whom we first met in 1992, stayed in England and took the opportunity to move into our home to be with our son Richard. The two boys being together brought much cheerful banter and joy into our lives and they didn't waste an opportunity to tease Paul and I unmercifully at most meal times.

As the days passed, our little old car was piled high with Ruza's personal luggage. Elaine, a co-worker and I set out from Yorkshire to drive Ruza on her return journey across Europe. Eight days later, in order to get back to Sarajevo, the route necessitated me driving the last two days over snow covered mountain tracks from Petrovac in the little old V.W Polo.

With lack of wisdom on my part, we had started the journey far too late in the day, the snow was still falling in soft flakes and we soon realised there was no way back from the treacherous single-track ridge of the mountain.

Hours later and when more or less at the summit, we came across a Muslim checkpoint where we were confronted with the familiar words.

"You go no further." We were inclined to agree, but knew we

could not have turned the car around in the snow even if we had wanted. Reversing several miles with my spinal problem was out of the question so Ruza came to the rescue and turned on the charm.

"My friend's from England," she seemed to say, much to their delight.

"We big friend in England. Riad Terzic," was their enthusiastic response. Immediately we were home and dry, the boy who had been saved under our mattress had been their school friend, and Ricki's fame had gone before us. Again God had placed His angels in position, and we were allowed to take a route that was banned to all civilians at the time.

After two further days of cramped uncomfortable travel we eventually arrived in what can only be described as a scene of desolation; the whole town was just a deserted, ransacked, concrete shell.

Although in shock at what she was seeing, Ruza insisted on walking up the main street on her own. Elaine and I followed in the car at a respectful distance behind her. Our challenge was to negotiate the craters left in the tarmac from exploded shells and grenades. Household rubbish was piled at least three metres high, everything from pots and pans and broken dolls lay forgotten amongst the rotting, rain sodden personal effects. Every shop building on both sides of the main street had been ransacked, burned or in some cases completely blown up. The further we followed the lady's footsteps the more one could feel her heart sink amongst the devastation. Were these the same streets, once lined with rose bushes where she had previously promenaded with her lady friends in past sultry summer evenings?

A little further on we were all delighted to find one small coffee shop open. For the first time in my life I welcomed going into a smoke filled atmosphere to meet the only inhabitants of the town. Ruza clearly knew all the men present as personal friends. As befitting her status, she was being treated with due respect, but my concern was, could these men stay close enough to protect her? Was this to be her home for the rest of her life? She had just left the security and comfort of England, to return to a destroyed town with no infrastructure, where she hoped she could make a real difference as a schoolteacher in the rebuilding of the lives of future children. But where could one woman start with no protection? Thankfully, there was the covering of her late husband's good name and memory, but in these circumstances this may not be enough.

It had been her late husband, Meho who had first instigated Deni and Mujo asking for help from us 'the English people'. Now, how could the English people be part of the rebuilding of a peaceful process?

Having absorbed the devastation and conferred with the few men of the town, Ruza was now ready to face the fateful time of returning to what had previously been her own apartment.

Elaine and I crawled out of the cramped car to join our friend on the grass verge outside her apartment block. Only then, without her realising it, we saw Ruza was standing next to an unexploded shell. Neither of us panicked, taking the view that the shell had remained safe until we arrived and there was no reason to suppose our presence would activate it now. Elaine and I made eye contact as we moved forward positioning ourselves each side of Ruza so we could guide her safely away. We were already beginning to catch the 'that's just the way it is' disease.

In greater trepidation we climbed the filthy, urinated, cold concrete steps. Although it was out of context, Ruza's front door was still in place on its hinges. The door even had a 'Claim of Ownership' sign, printed in Meho's name by order of the town's

Police. Given the door was not locked and fearing it may be booby trapped, we dared to enter slowly. The whole place was desecrated. Every piece of furniture had either been destroyed or used as a toilet. Her kitchen had been completely ripped out, and every piece of sanitary ware in her bathroom had been smashed to pieces. Even the water pipes had been ripped out, with every electric switch ripped from the walls along with all connected wiring.

We moved in a state of shock into the second bedroom. The scene was made all the more poignant as we spotted Deni's school report from five years previous, still on the windowsill. The only possession left from what had been a comfortable and affluent life style.

How could we leave our friend here? But eventually, leave her we must as all her bridges back to England had been burned. This was to be her new life. No man to protect her, no real home, no income other than what we could offer from our faithful supporters. Her only comfort, the comfort of the Saviour within her own heart; if ever she needed a friend in Jesus, she certainly needed him now.

It ripped us apart to leave her in such circumstances, but if we were to be of any practical help to her and the other thousands who would return, then we knew the work needed to carry on.

CHAPTER 17

A Touch of the Emotions

There are many thousands of people in England who have given their 'widows mite' in support of making our missions possible. We know their 'love gifts' without doubt have saved lives.

There is no person from either ethnic group in the Balkans with whom we have spoken, who is not carrying a deep pain etched within. Each has an ache, where their heart has been ripped apart, savaged by loss and broken in two. The pain is so deep; words cannot describe the intensity.

There is a grief, which cuts like a knife and has a stranglehold, which stretches human endurance and daily survival to the limits. Death at times would be a welcome relief.

There is a hopelessness, which can consume the human spirit in a pit of despair. There is an Evil, which is so corrupt and dark, from which we all try to run, which eats away at the very souls of mankind.

The people in the Balkans have experienced all of this. They have been raped, tortured but worst of all, at times ignored.

"Don't they care?" is the continued cry from within their broken hearts. Governments have made and sold the landmines, then sent food to help the children with the blown off limbs. Man's inhumanity to man is incomprehensible and these people have learned, however sharp or long the ordeal within the human soul, there can be no terms of compromise. Peace within is the only real peace.

Paul and I became used to carrying the pain of these people in our hearts, but never more than when Ricki had been living with us in England for nine months, did we attempt to action a mission with so much forethought and prayerful deliberation. For the first time we found ourselves more personally and emotionally involved.

During this period Ricki had been one of God's great blessings to us. There are no words to describe our love towards him along with many more of 'our boys' whom we met along the way. Anyone visiting our home has much difficulty in distinguishing which of 'the boys' is our own son.

Richard has been fantastic and we are really proud of the way he opened up his own heart to receive Ricki and Deni as instant brothers. Over the months we had been carefully photographing every 'normal' activity for Ricki's parents, believing one day we would have the pleasure of being able to reassure them of his well being. So, by the end of January 1994 after surviving, yet again, four arduous weeks to reach Zenica, we were delighted when at last we were going to meet Ricki's family once more. What I was not looking forward to experiencing was the anticipated emotional part of the reunion. Both Paul and I had been a witness to some very emotional situations and somehow whilst in the midst of it, in order to have been of service, we had managed to keep our own emotions battened down. Now finding ourselves in this situation, I wasn't sure if I could handle being in the middle of the expected highly charged atmosphere.

When we were finally united with the people of central Bosnia again, we were totally unprepared for the great changes since the previous time we met. People, who six months ago were able to keep afloat, were now sinking into a sea of despair. An air of desperation hung over the town. Our lovely hospital director gazed at us with a glazed look emanating from his gaunt face. He was like a candle that had been snuffed out. The light had gone out of him and he was only a shadow of his former self.

As we unloaded sacks of flour and rice for the hospital off our lorry, we noticed an elderly man had carefully gathered up the few grains of rice that had fallen out of a sack; he then gently placed the precious morsels in his pocket.

We moved apprehensively on to the school where the large crowds soon swamped us, pushing and shoving in desperate attempts to obtain food. People begged and pleaded frantically, some stealing whatever they could as we pretended not to notice. We were emotionally distressed by our inability to meet the needs of all. How inadequate we felt. We could never be satisfied with the little we were able to offer and we shared the people's sense of panic.

However we did know we were bringing some hope, the fact that we were still getting through seemed little consolation at the time but, it did reinforce what they saw as their only hope. For Paul and I, the hardest part was always feeling we were not doing enough when measured by the need, but one thing I have learnt is, if we will do our best then we can rely on God to do the rest.

I remember well one time we parked Sidney, our new lorry, just outside a Muslim/Serb front line. I learnt later that snipers at a two-mile distance could have finished us off along with our British lorry with no trouble at all. So on this occasion we loaded a few boxes of bandages and dressings, which we had perceived to be a pittance, into the boot of an old car and took the risk of speeding them in a crazy zig–zag motion into one small town, a few miles just out of Sarajevo where Meho had advised of great need.

We were taken to the Commander of the troops and were amazed to discover the only medical facilities for a whole regiment were three crepe bandages which had been used several times. I remember whipping myself for the pittance that we had brought thinking that maybe we were insulting the whole army.

Thankfully, I remembered my own reply to my eldest son Michael when he asked, "Mum, why are you going again? Aren't there plenty of men much stronger than you? Is your going really making a difference?" On hearing his apprehension and the emotional cost to our family who continually waited for news of us, I found all I could do was answer.

"Maybe you are right, yes there are soldiers and male aid workers who are much stronger than me, but if our going makes a difference to just one mother, for her son, then I think… that could be my son."

Imagine therefore our joy when a few months later, we received a letter from a young man who had escaped from Sarajevo and whom we were able to help to safety a few months earlier. He wrote from America.

"You people gave me hope. For three years I had lived, having given up all hope and belief that there was any goodness left in the world with the exception of my parents, but you two came along and I have changed in my heart. Through your faith you have given me hope and a new life."

Four years later, I did actually meet his mother and father. They proudly showed me a photograph of their son being met at an American airport; I just burst into uncontrollable tears of gratitude and thanks to God. I had no idea that I was still carrying this young man in my heart who, but for the grace of God, could have been my son. He remains in my heart.

Now we were back in central Bosnia again, one of the few aid lorries to get through and I was heading straight for Ricki's parents. Paul was doing some last minute deliveries of food parcels sent by refugees' families in England. We were their 'Postman Pat', their only bridge. Encouraged by a file full of letters from relatives expressing deep appreciation, we were compelled to continue the missions long after sense or reason told us to stop.

I made my way to the upper classroom at the end of the corridor. It had been Ricki's parents and brothers' home, along with twenty others for over a year. I soon tuned into Ricki's mother's gentle, calm way and was anxious to give her the carefully prepared photo album of Ricki's new life. Within the pages were scenes of unimaginable joy, in direct contrast to the family's gloomy depravation. I had been able to appreciate the sordid conditions and daily fears, which had led Ricki's mother to literally entrust her son's life into the hands of complete strangers. These photos were meant to bring her pleasure so that she would know her trust in God's providence had been well placed.

We could now both share in the fruit of her courage by letting him go. Smiling I gently offered her the gift, miming the actions of taking photos and at the same time pointing to my watch, hoping she would open the gift at a later time as emotions were running high. We women were only just hanging onto any sense of decorum when Ricki's father pushed his son's sheepskin coat towards me. Ricki had already told me about his favourite coat which had been the only possession he had been able to save when they fled their home at gunpoint. I felt I knew it well.

"No problem," I smiled, receiving the coat with hands outstretched. Then his mother indicated a gift for me personally. The gentle lady had lovingly crocheted a white lace tablecloth and if that was not remarkable enough I was later to discover that she had made it by crocheting all of it with a piece of bent wire.

Still trying to express her eternal gratitude further, Ricki's mother then took a ring from her own finger and forced it onto mine. The tears were beginning to well up to near overflowing, but neither of us would let go. I turned to the interpreter nearby. "Please tell her, thank you, but I will only wear the ring until the day Ricki gets married, then I will give it to his bride."

This remark opened the floodgates of tears and pent up emotions; despite my determination I could hold out no longer and in the heat of the moment turned myself away only to be caught in the arms of Ricki's six foot, handsome youngest brother. Instinctively his strong arms opened, he smiled a broad open smile and I could do no more than collapse, caught securely in his young compassionate arms. Weeks of tension came flooding out in deep unfettered sobs; mascara ran in a torrent of tears over my flushed cheeks as I tried to hide my embarrassment.

"Oh good gracious this will never do. Look at me, this is ridiculous!" I hastily wiped my face on the back of my hand and struggled to regain my composure as the beautiful family joined me crying and smiling.

I poked in my pockets but never a tissue when one really needs it. I tried desperately to wipe away the mascara, but the father's arms reached out also wanting to hug this person few ever get to see. His thick dark rimmed glasses held together with brown tape, did nothing to hide his love and compassion and even in the middle of a war I knew I was totally safe and secure.

CHAPTER 18

The Formation of 'Holy Ground Mission in Faith'

For nearly a year and a half I had been writing and re-writing the Ricki part of this story, whilst at the same time Paul and I had continued our 3,000 mile round trips, made possible by the support of an ever growing number of people back home.

There was a stage when I thought the book was finished until a lady in Ireland said, on reading the draft manuscript.

"Well yes, but what has happened since? Come on Jacqui, there must be more; I have an instinct that you haven't even begun to tell the whole story yet."

How could I answer the Irish lady's question since the story was still being lived? But yes, maybe another book later.

Paul and I believe it is not enough to play ones part at a time when the war situation is high profile. Indeed, it takes the extra quality of endurance and faithfulness to continue in the long term, supporting the rebuilding process long after the media hype has ceased.

I know that I am not in a position at this time to write the final chapter of the work which Paul and I have been privileged to pioneer. I expect somewhere in the future we can only live it. So instead, I'll try and bring this very small portion of God's story up to date with the events from March 1996.

*****

At least for that time, gone was the emergency work of those war years and gradually over a period of time, we found ourselves more and more moved towards strengthening our support base in order to extend the 'Humanitarian Aid' part of our calling.

For two years Eileen, my prayer partner, and latterly Elaine, a retired school teacher, and I had spent much time spiritually listening and working through the 'inner nudges' until we believed we had understood many of the lessons we were being taught. We carefully measured our experiences and then checked them through with the word of God.

Paul and I always needed to return to England to raise the necessary funds, so when home, we quite simply told of the need and trusted God to move hearts in support.

Thanks to the ongoing financial gifts from all manner of people within our neighbourhood, schools and local churches; within two months we were able to return to Ruza and the growing population.

Again we completed the 1500 miles over land and sea, and this time with two full lorries, seven other vehicles, and twenty-one people all armed with paintbrushes, school equipment, food, general aid and a lot of talent and energy, all willing to give generously.

In the following four-week period, ten rooms were painted in the maternity block of the hospital at Petrovac. Three large rooms in the secondary school at Ilijas, and five rooms in a small school where Ruza was about to start teaching. Today in that same town there are approximately 4/5,000 children and 12,000 people, mostly refugees from Srebrenicia and Zepa towns which saw unbelievable atrocities. These people may look 'normal,' but each person has their own heart wrenching and ugly inner scars, which are unlikely to heal unless a climate of forgiveness comes into play. Given the political history of the country, that could be centuries away, which makes the need for unconditional love so important our hope is that lives can be healed in a climate where God's Holy presence can be invited.

To that end, little did we realise that another piece on the chessboard was coming into play. At a time of distributing food, clothes and shoes from the back of our lorry, I managed to pull a child on board who was being crushed in the surge of the excitement. To my shame, I became conscious of taking a pace backwards, as the smell from the little one hit my unsuspecting senses. Immediately I looked around for clean clothes to fit him, but every box of clothes we had on the surface inside the lorry was much too small. By passing a food box outside the lorry we discovered the child was with his elderly grandfather who had been doing his best to look after him since all three of his sons had vanished during the war.

The following day, after much reconnaissance, Ruza, Elaine and I were at the so called Mayor's office.

"Please give us that building for God's work." I was referring to a building, which had been a Medical Centre before the war. Although badly damaged, in my mind's eye, I could already see the building fitted ready for children. In fact it would provide a home for one particular child and his grandfather, who I definitely knew needing bathing.

The eighteen-roomed building had neither windows or doors, no water pipes or electricity; all the wiring had been ripped out. It had no toilets or sanitation of any kind, yet still I could see its wonderful potential.

"How can I give you that building?" The small sincere man protested against my onslaught.

"Who else will bathe this child if we don't?" I continued with no punches spared. The poor man had his finger to the temple of his head, trying to make sense of what was being asked, so he enquired further.

"What makes you people tick? I hear many good things about you, but I don't understand you." Now scratching his head trying to work through his own thoughts.

"Before the war I was a Godly man" the Mayor continued, "My wife died in my arms, then the war came, and I went to the front line, and killed many people." Now he was bowing his head with tears in his eyes, in shame. "Now I don't know what to do."

Immediately my tone changed; gently and quietly I continued to speak:

"Thankfully God knows your heart and we have come to bring you and the people of your town good news." I began to speak with an anointing that could only have come from the Holy Spirit. Elaine began to pray in support. The presence of God began to fill the dark ugly room.

"You are not proud of what you have done. You have a humble heart. Well, the Jesus we serve has died on the cross for all our sins and our Heavenly Father wants us to accept him into our hearts, and then receive complete forgiveness. Would you like us to pray with you?" I dared to ask. Ruza who was interpreting took a big breath. I could see she found the whole conversation quite an unequivocal experience to be happening right in the heart of Islam. We continued as the Spirit of God gave utterance as the humble man opened his heart and prayed for forgiveness. He asked Jesus Christ to become his personal Saviour. We were to learn later that this man had been one of the leaders in the local mosque before the war.

Eventually the Mayor came to learn that Paul and I were the

English people whom he had heard about. We had driven an ambulance to the front line, as a gift to his regiment. He also discovered it was Paul and I who had brought much needed medical dressings in the boot of a car, right in the middle of the fighting. Apparently the Mayor knew first hand that those few dressings and pain killers had served well his friends who were taking heavy casualties. We also came to see that those two simple acts would become the cement in the foundations for us to serve in the town. Six months later we were leased the building for five years.

Paul and I became the founder members of the 'Holy Ground Mission' a pioneering 'Mission in Faith', which would give lay people like us, the opportunity to discover and work out our own faith, whilst at the same time serving within a structure, which seeks to be faithful to the New Testament principles of discipleship.

After all the legal registrations were done in England and Bosnia we each began to develop in new ways through the work and witness, and as usual all growth was painful. One of the first battles we needed to confront was our own unworthiness as leaders. We needed to look carefully at our own personal call in discipleship and balance that with the perceived understanding within the structured church of how leaders are ordained. The question of administering communion out in the mission field was an area I needed personally to feel comfortable with before the Lord. It was then, that I heard about a candidate for ordination who was asked by the credentials committee: "Would you be disappointed if we did not ordain you this year?"

He replied. "Oh no, God has already ordained me, he's just waiting for you guys to get the paperwork done."

With that point settled and our commissioning service in England behind us, we decided to send out an edited version of the writings of C.T.Studd 1861-1931, founder of the World Evangelisation Crusade.

Whilst we in the Mission were not making an attack on the Established Church, we were certainly moved at the time against the apathy which we 'Christians' sometimes give out as spiritual confetti. The clichés help us to sit more comfortably unmoved against Satan's negative thought provoking attack within ourselves, our families and our marriages. They perpetuate the constant evil which we continually label as 'somebody else's fault'. We form part of our society and we can so easily be the conduit for the negative spirit. If as Missionaries and co-workers we are to be effective in our calling, then we need to be vigilant in confession of our own sin. Sin is first about ownership, taking responsibility and accountability. There can be no escape against the final judgement.

C.T. Charles Studd wrote:-

Christ's call is to feed the hungry, not the full:
To save the lost not the stiff-necked; not to call scoffers but sinners to repentance.
Not to build and furnish comfortable churches in which to rock Christian professors to sleep, by means of stereotyped prayers and artistic musical performances, but to raise up living churches of souls from amongst the destitute.
To capture men from the devil's clutches and snatch them from the very jaws of hell, to enlist them into an Almighty Army of God.
This can only be accomplished by a red-hot Holy Ghost religion where neither Church, State or traditions are worshiped or preached but only Christ and Him Crucified.
It's experience not preaching that hurts the devil and confounds the world.
The training is not that of the schools but of the market place.

It's the hot free heart that knocks the devil out.

Nothing than fork-lightening Christians will count. A lost reputation is the best degree for Christ's sake.

The difficulty is to believe that God can use scallywags as us, but of cause he wants faith and fools rather than talents and culture.

All God wants is a heart, any old turnip will do for a head, so long as we are empty for then He fills us with the Holy Ghost.

Nail your colours of Christ to the mast and do it now! For the sake of the work He has given us to do, the evangelisation of the un-evangelised.

Christ does not want nibblers of the possible... but grabbers of the impossible by faith and wisdom from the Almighty Saviour who gave the command.

Is there a wall in our path?... Then leap over it.

Are there loins and scorpions in our way?... We will trample them underfoot!

Soldiers of Jesus! Never surrender! Nail your colours to the mast!

Can we listen to these words of an African pastor and will we make them ours?

"I'm part of the fellowship of the unashamed. The die has been cast because I've already stepped over the line. I'm a disciple of His and won't look back, let up, slow down, back away or be still.

My past is redeemed, my present makes sense and my future is secure. I am finished with low living, sight walking, small planning, colourless dreams, and cheap living with dwarfed goals.

I no longer need pre-eminence, plaudits or popularity. I don't have to be right, first, tops, praised, regarded or rewarded. I now live by faith, walk by patience, lift my prayers and labour in His power.

I won't give up, shut up, let up, until I have stayed up, stored up, prayed up, paid up and preached up the cause of Christ. I must go till

He comes, give till I drop. Preach till all know, and work till He stops me. And when he comes for His own, He'll have no problem recognising me-for my banner will be clear."

By late 1996 until 2002 the Mission Centre became an oasis in the middle of a spiritual desert. It is a home for many children who are fed and clothed daily. It is a Humanitarian Aid Distribution Centre for over 2,000 of the town's inhabitants, hardly any of whom have work. In addition, it is a home for the dying where the Gospel message is preached through our daily lives.

Even today as I look back it still seems an impossible task that so few people could have established a Mission Centre in Faith whilst at the same time continuing to commute back to England, in order to raise the financial support for the ongoing work. With no government or official funding, the missions' work is still run on faith. We know every gift given to keep the work of the mission alive, is a direct result of God moving the hearts of His people and for that we continue to praise Him!

Continuously over the years, one cry would always be heard from my lips. "Lord send us your people with hearts like lions, who are sold out for Christ Jesus." We realise that the gospel message can only be brought alive as the Spirit of God moves through the faith of His people in action.

However we must be vigilant. One of the dangers is that we become distracted from our first call of delivering the message of forgiveness, as we endeavour to fulfil the physical work with too few hands; we could become a blunt sword.

The daily work has been, and no doubt will continue to be, extremely exacting. These extracts from our Day Logs show why we need 'sold out' long-term missionaries:

Friday, May 16, 1997. JR

The physical work on the building is hard, mostly for the men. Paul and Frank have spent their first weeks in this building, without windows or doors, battling against the cold. They wash their paintbrushes in the melted snow off the side of the hill. However, for Ruza and I there is no greater battle than trying to get through the oppressing bureaucracy. The customs officials want the weight of every knife, fork and spoon weighed and recorded, and considering the lorry's six ton load, there is no way we are prepared to play that game.

The whole system has a root of fear, a few keeping control over the masses. It seems nobody will take final responsibility for saying 'yes'. The goal posts are constantly moved, and it seems, the game is to send a person from one department to another until one is worn down into complete submission. Most people simply give up.

I'm confident that as we have already, by the grace of God, been able to get this work established in the heart of the people, whilst at the same time planting it in the heart of the individual Churches, then the Mission long term can become an excellent training ground for committed future leaders. This work is so desperately needed for the 'little people' at the bottom of the pecking order where little free help ever penetrates.

We must keep alert to the wiles of the enemy because right from the start we are challenging Satan's stronghold. It is easy to buckle under the pressure of a lot of people who think they have the right to demand that their needs be met. Victory can only be won through prayer, patience and endurance. It is a time to dig in and hold the line.

Saturday, May 17, 1997. JR

It's 2.30 a.m. Having had little sleep, I continue to lie on my bed wrestling with the demons of darkness. With this machine, writing has become my emotional outlet. It's where I can lay down all my thoughts as if on an open table.

Afternoon: One very thin lady along with a ten-year-old boy has come for any help she can get. Both are riddled with fleas and I suspect she has come for money. She is like someone out of Belson and again I suspect with a drink problem, which is confirmed later. I invite them both for a meal; she indicates all she eats comes back up. I know she is right. How can we help? I feel a million miles away, but in a moment our eyes meet and she senses my heart towards her. Tears are softly shed; an extra warmth permeates the whole building, she is much loved.

Monday, May 19, 1997. JR

To our real joy, two grubby children appear for the second time. They are happy to be washed and fitted with new socks and shoes, and receive a second dose of vitamins. We are in desperate need of flea powder for them. I don't think the customs will allow me back into England unless we get this problem solved or I spend six months in quarantine. As the shower is not yet fitted we bath them outside in the sun. They have faces of Angels and I love them already.

Meho is one of those children who, when he gives you a smile speaks volumes. In just two days I have seen him blossom from a frightened little mouse into an impish happy child. He is already established well into all our affections.

May 21, 1997. JR

I have discovered a British police officer. What a joy to meet the people who are doing the real work at ground floor level. He is going to have a word with a Gunman counterpart. He told me to expect flea powder at 9am tomorrow. I would not have believed I could have got excited about anything so mundane.

July 8, 1997 On Duty Pete and JR

Pete has taken spectacles up the hill to complete yesterday's commitment. His morning was a great success. He went on another visit to take shoes, bread and tomatoes. Boots for another man along with more spectacles for Tomo, the man with the stroke. Just a few pairs of spectacles tucked in my personal luggage have gone a long way. Pete also had a good time of ministry with the man in the wheelchair. I thank God for him, he has done an excellent job.

It is raining and we are besieged with about forty children. Ladies from yesterday are insisting on receiving everything. They hover. I am sad to say greed not need, exists. I openly pray in front of them. Tongues are a powerful gift in such situations. I feel I need six pairs of hands.

We are asked to visit a lady who is near to death. She has open wounds; I clean them and do my best. I thank God because she is much loved by her family.

Afternoon: We visit a camp fifty miles away of refugees whom we have been feeding for the last three years. Just to see their faces was a joy. By the time we return we are very tired and decide on light food.

10 p.m.: *Ruza arrives in heavy rain to say she has been trying to calm her neighbour and can we help. The lady is a Serb. She claims someone is trying to kill her. (Not surprising she is frightened. She is one of only a handful of Serbs in town.) She says she wants to see her children just once before she dies. We have contacted both children. Neither is prepared to come. We bring her into the mission for the night; I sat in her room quietly singing until the early hours.*

August 3, 1997.

A Soldier from the Bosnia Army came to thank Paul and the

Mission for helping the children in Ilijas, especially as his sister's daughter is now ill in hospital. He was on the front line during the war and despite all the horrors; he came across as a gentle good-hearted man, a deep thinker, not bitter but philosophical. He feels the soldiers have recovered very quickly from their experiences of war and the recovery would be even quicker if the economy was in a better state. He expressed the view that during the war they had a focus to survive; now there is no focus, no goals and no purpose. Living here is like walking constantly on a rumbling earthquake.

December 19, 1997. JR

What an unbelievable morning. After a very deep time of communion with our Precious Lord it was as if the gates of Heaven opened. People flooded in for help, yet in an uncharacteristic orderly way. They had so many varied needs yet the Holy Spirit totally ministered His wonderful grace and presence. So much deep healing. If this were my only day here in the Mission Centre for the rest of my life, then I would be satisfied. It was just as if all I had to do was raise my hands in adoration of Him and He sent down the rivers of healing love.

At one time there must have been twelve people in the room all waiting expectantly and no one went away wanting or disappointed. The Holy Spirit ministered in full power. His presence was confirmed by the fact that at the same time of ministry there must have been over forty children playing happily feet away and another nineteen adults came in for spectacles.

One lady came for pills for anxiety, depression and the like. I refused saying I would not give her a plaster to cover the blockage within. Everyone else sat around stunned. Some nodded in agreement, especially one very young lady, whom I am told is an alcoholic. For two hours she has just sat here and fed off the teaching, which I was able to share. Silver and gold have I none but in the name of Jesus Christ... receive.

The wonderful thing about this work is; one does not have to be wise, wealthy or clever, anyone can step out in whatever amount of faith they possess and be channels of blessing for his neighbour.

Monday, January 12, 1998. JR

A slow start to the day because of the black smog, which hangs over the town like a thick blanket. The cold, grey day is brightened by the children's laughter coming from our playroom. I am pleased that one mother has remembered to bring her daughter for her second dose of worm medicine.

The people begin to be drawn into the warmth of this building, most gathering around my desk as if it were a magnet. Some come just to sit and absorb the atmosphere, others come to lay just a little more of their grief out to be heard and held. Some come with hope that this place may be the answer to their prayers.

One old man wait's about an hour for the opportunity to show me a photograph of his son whom he lost in the war. An average, good-looking fourteen year old boy in his blue and white football strip. It's easy to be with him.

A young couple came with their year old son, trusting they could have ongoing help. The mother is nine months pregnant yet looks only six months because of malnutrition. I give them a cot, blankets, sheets, nappies, pins, rubber pants, baby clothes, talc, vaseline, shampoo; all their Christmases at once, but before they leave, I lift a pair of scissors and mime to the young husband a certain operation. The ladies gathered and smile in agreement.

A well-dressed young lady asks for some help for a certain female problem. I take a deep breath and count age on my side as an asset as I try to do my best.

In the middle of it all a tidy middle-aged man comes in quite urgently wanting to be seen. We take him in to our little medical room where we discover his back badly burned. He says he had a fit and fell onto an electric fire a week ago. The whole area of flesh is charred and by this time well infected. The name 'Jesus' comes out of my lips as I quietly wonder about the pain he has already been through without help.

"You must go to doctors" I advise. He laughs a soft laugh at my stupidity.

"No money, no doctor," he replies embarrassed. We do our best.

In five hours I have witnessed the varied spectrum of colourful human nature. It is here to be discovered, experienced and tenderly carried each morning of the week.

"Jacqui, cuppa tea?"

"Yes please," is my natural response as I wonder why I am feeling so drained when it's only two o' clock in the afternoon.

CHAPTER 19

The Birth of Hospice Care in Bosnia

By March 1998 a doctor from the local medical centre was asking if we would take in two cancer patients for care. I knew right from the very beginning we would all be in for a steep learning curve, and I would probably be called upon to walk the extra mile, but I also knew 'His grace would be sufficient.'

Immediately the local paid staff went into revolt from their fears and prejudices. If I would dare to take these people into the mission, they certainly would not go into the same room and clean. Regardless of the verbal pressure from the local staff, beds were moved and prepared for the new arrivals, everything was well in place.

By mid-afternoon we were ready to receive our first patients. The first was half way up the path on a stretcher before my attention was called to supervise the blanket covered lump that was to reveal an emaciated skeleton, curled up in the foetal position. I took a deep breath to find the inner strength and authority, which went into action straight away. The hospital staffs were delighted and most reassured, which in turn gave me the much-needed encouragement.

The second man, Shefco, walked in wearing his Sunday suit with a huge lump on the side of his neck. Immediately I knew him. He had been in before and I recognised him as the man who waited to show me the photograph of one of his sons. I had seen his inner dignity and respected the way he had quietly observed life around him. This man runs deep and I was sure we would get on well together.

Ruza was quite rightly concerned as to how I would cope alone at night and urged me to find a trained nurse to help.

"No Ruza, I need to discover what is needed first. Give me just one night, then I will know so very much more and will be able to decide which way to move."

I instinctively knew the first thing I needed to do was to make some real contact with the first soul who had come in on the stretcher. I knelt on my knees by his bed to be at his level, so I could make eye contact. As I stroked his face he opened his eyes; a way out look at first, then it happened, we connected and he knew he was safe. I saw the twinkle in his eye.

We need twice as many pillows in the building, I thought, and if we had backrests, then that would make things a lot easier. Thankfully I knew just the right man in England. I was sure Mr. Todd, one of our staunch supporters, would soon make some designed like deck chairs.

The town's chief nurse came to fit the drips trying to use our overhead heating pipes instead of a medical stand, but with the collapsed veins she finally had to give in and fetch a precious stand from their meagre level of equipment. Next came the catheter for the urine and I have to say I was more than delighted to have to empty a bag, rather than sleep next to what I knew was the special smell reserved to take away man's dignity.

The whole exercise seemed to take hours before our new arrivals were a little more comfortable and it looked safe enough for me to dare try for some sleep in the next room.

The next three nights became an education. No one interested in human nature should be without these experiences. I already knew that within most male bodies there is a little boy still trying to get his mother's attention. It was truly amazing to me, how even when one was at death's door, racked with pain, unable to move off a bed, one could find so many ways of testing the love of a complete stranger. But test it he did, systematically over the next three nights.

I soon discovered I needed to forget about having neat, tucked in corners on sheets. The smooth sheets were pulled straight off along with the protective rubber by the patient. I decided to give in gracefully and wrap the skeleton covered with skin in a duvet and pretend I had been that wise in the first place. At the same time, I removed the lighter, which had been hidden under the pillow to accompany the much-needed national drug. Yet, by 2am my suspicions were well founded as I followed my nose. Yes, between them they had managed to beat the system. Four dog ends had been stubbed out onto the bedside cabinet.

"You naughty boy," came out of my mouth almost like a verbal torrent of gushing water, but in a flash I knew it was only a game, and I had better let them win.

"I'll have your tail off for you if you don't watch out," knowing full well neither could understand a word I was saying, but I was sure they both knew something I didn't.

All through the night, at a rate of every fifteen minutes, I continued to stumble out of bed in the dark, trying to find the elusive slipper and the sleeve of the dressing gown, which always seemed to get inside out.

Morning brought perfect sleep to the two babes and strangely enough I was not at all tired, which is not what I would have expected of my own nature.

As one particular member of Bosnian staff arrived, I knew I

was headed for trouble the moment she came in through the door. She did not see why she should have to look after old men and proceeded to carry the rest of the team with her.

"What's your real problem?" I tried to encourage, trying to get at the truth.

"I don't want to be near them. We could catch what they have. I'm scared," she blurted.

"Now, that's understandable. However, tell me, what would you have me do with these men, let them die alone?" I confronted, as gently as I could but without compromise. I knew however, that her fear had disturbed the loving balance in the routine work. I chose to understand her fears but, why was I not surprised when the doctor came and the infusions would not go in through the veins?

All along I could sense the anger in our second patient. He was well justified in feeling angry having witnessed his wife being burnt alive by his neighbour along with his two cows and home. How could we not love him and comfort him as best we were able?

I believed the ladies would rise to the new situation. I had seen their hearts, and somehow, I was going to pick them up and carry them for a while, at least until the dust settled.

Saturday night brought very much the same pattern from the men. Constant groaning from one in deep pain and a continual need for the spittoon from the other. Meanwhile, in the dark I tried my best to rustle the sheets over my ears at the appointed moments of release.

Next, from my bed I could hear strange ripping sounds coming from the sick room. Quietly I waited, hoping for a clue as to the new test that was being set before me. The sounds from the room quietened; I crept in to see if I could guess the new game. In the dark I could clearly see something white. The little tyke had systematically pulled all fifty rubber gloves out of a new box, and I presume, joyfully scattered them over the floor as far as his strength would allow. I could not believe anybody in that condition could be so mischievous. No, I would not blow. This was only a test, a mere game.

Smiling inside I snuggled down into my small bed for prayer. I claimed every inch of ground in Jesus' name. God rained his grace down from heaven and gave me such an overflowing love for these men. Victoriously I claimed them for the Kingdom of Heaven for all eternity. Nothing would break my love for them, regardless of how much they tried to set me up.

Sunday was physically hard and the constant night duty after long days was beginning to take its toll. I did the best I could with a Sunday service in between constant sick room duty and wondered where the rest of the churches were.

In the early hours of Monday morning I was beckoned over to the bed. My little boy was hungry. Could I believe, at 4.20am in the morning and almost without a breath in his body, he wanted bread? I fetched the manna and we sat on the bed together as he ate like someone who was now at the banquet of heaven.

"Have I just seen what I have seen?" I was sure this was the supernatural strength, which comes before death. Rather like a pregnant woman getting a burst of energy and cleaning the house just before labour pains begin. I could of course be wrong, so I listened astutely for the rest of the night.

Morning brought the usual constant stream of people needing food and medical help. By 11.30am I had dealt with twenty-four requests for food to everybody's complete satisfaction.

Then a social worker came to check upon our patients. Shamefully both Ruza and I bloomed with pride at how strong our first soul was getting, describing some of the antics of the previous night. Still with pride and satisfaction, we walked confidently into the room.

"Come on treasure. What are you doing down in the bed like that?" I moved to straighten him up. His hand was on the side rail as if he was trying to get up. I stopped in my tracks as Ruza's words penetrated my skull.

"He's dead."

She's right, I thought, but disbelieved my own eyes. Slowly I moved to stroke his forehead, then fell to my knees to look at him from a different angle in the hope that with a change of direction, the view might reveal a different picture. Then as if programmed, I walked quietly around to the other side of the bed and put on rubber gloves without even thinking. I straightened him up whilst at the same time beckoning to the other patient to leave the room and against my principles, go and have a cigarette.

We closed down the reception and made sure the children were all safely out of view to all the comings and goings. One of the ladies immediately came forward and helped me lay out the body in the nice clean sheet, which we had put on the bed only half an hour before.

"I'm so glad we had put a lovely new shirt on him. Didn't he look sweet?" I rejoiced that my little boy was going home looking smart.

Alone, I said my farewells. Again, I claimed his soul entreating the Father's mercy in Jesus' name. I did not know what else to do except take time for a silent personal tear.

Bedtime brought a flood of loneliness for me. In much physical pain, I climbed into bed. Where was Paul? Fifteen hundred miles away. The best I could do was to get his dressing gown off the back of the door, put it around my back and pull the sleeve over my shoulder for a bit of comfort at the end of the day. The one thing of which I was sure, the little tyke did know something I didn't know. He had succeeded to get right under my skin, and he had made his way straight into this old heart, that Jesus gave.

By August 1998 we had an urgent call from Bosnia because our second cancer patient was in the final stages and desperately needed pain relief. We are ever thankful at the wonderful way in which our mighty God moved at that dreadful time.

I sat in front of my open Bible with my heart tumbling out thoughts not knowing if I could even put together words that could convey the need out in Bosnia for that one poor man and many thousands like him.

My own logic and torrents of thoughts felt irresponsible at the least. My brain was telling me… '*You can't just up sticks and fly to the other side of the world in response to every need.*' Yet, I knew deep in my heart the sin would be *not* to take some action.

At that moment I could only do as I had done in the past, that was to lay out the problem openly, then trust the Father to move the chess pieces in that current situation.

By eight o' clock that night I had an unprecedented urge to go and collect some work from a lady who had previously offered help, but who had been restricted because she had needed to nurse her brother who had just died of cancer.

Paul suggested that we eat first, but I knew that I would be weak enough not to respond to the quickening in my spirit if I dared to sit down and relax.

As soon as we arrived and without either of us saying a single word about Bosnia or Shefco's situation, the lady in question went up stairs and brought down a big bag. To our amazement she began to lay out boxes of half used pain killers onto the coffee table in front of us. We both knew that in six years of taking hundreds of tons of medical aid, nobody had ever given us so much. Only God in His infinite mercy could have brought this urgent help into our hands.

The following morning I checked with the police and then acquired the relevant clearance from the Home Office. By mid morning one of our missionaries, who had been on compassionate leave awaiting an operation, had phoned to say she had discovered that she had been missed off the waiting list, and that she had Shefco on her heart over the last week. She had wondered why this should be. When I was able to share the current situation with her, straight away she made herself available.

That same night four of us moved into the presence of our Heavenly Father in prayer. We all agreed that as God had provided the pain killers without us telling anybody of the need, then we could trust Him to provide the cost of the airfare to get them out to Shefco.

Having been challenged (tongue in cheek) by Paul the previous night for my lack of faith, I actually decided to book the ticket by phone first thing the following morning. While I still had the receiver in my hand, Paul having opened the mail rushed up the stairs to my desk with an air of excitement and triumph. He calmly put a cheque in front of me received from a blessed lady in Sheffield who knew nothing about the situation. She had been moved in her heart to give the mission half of her holiday money because she had not felt the need to go away.

Such blessedness! Such love!

What can we say but, '*Lord we love you… you blow our minds, your love is more precious than silver or gold.*' Can you imagine a God who cares that much about just one man in the middle of Bosnia? A God who thinks that man is precious enough to move heaven and earth to show His love for him and then in His grace to do it through people like us? Can we help but love Him?

I write this next testimony to share that no situation is impossible for a God who cares:

By mid summer 1998 we were sent a 'minder' in the form of a gentle giant who had been born in Sarajevo thirty-six years previously. He could speak German and English. His mother had taken him to Germany when he was eight years old, after his father had been killed on a railway line.

He hadn't been in Germany long before the young man found himself in bad company. Over the next years he started taking drugs and eventually, as a mature adult, found himself waking up from a drug overdose in prison.

At this time, the end of the Balkan war, the German authorities decided to deport all Bosnians back to Bosnia and, as he only had a Bosnian passport, found him about to be separated from his dear mother. Within days and with all his worldly possessions in two cardboard boxes under his arms, he found himself standing at Sarajevo airport in shock, unable to believe the devastation before him.

In time he was given a room and a mattress by the authorities, but he soon became hungry. Again he went to the authorities for help and a social worker told him to go and steal if he needed food.

Back in his room he looked out of the window onto the market place below and was tempted to go and steal food. Instead, he prayed to the God who gave him life, to take it from him and let him die. Not realising God had heard his cry he went for a walk around the town, passed the mission building and noticed Paul coming out whistling a song of praise. Approaching Paul, he asked for work. Paul, sensing a deep need, asked him to knock a small hole in a wall to make a hatch between the kitchen and a proposed new Hospice unit. Paul then paid the gentle giant, by giving him sugar, coffee, milk and a tin of corned beef to take home and prayed with him.

A week later I arrived and naturally invited the gentle giant for a meal where both Paul and I were able to share how he could have a clean slate and be forgiven of all his past sin. Tenderly he wept like a babe, spewing out all his pain until exhausted. Very gently we were able to pick him up and stand him on Holy Ground. Our friend Juso, now works in the mission and is fast becoming a great man of God, serving whoever he is able in the name of Jesus.

We don't know who gave us that corned beef but we do know God used it in a mighty way.

*****

One day our regular taxi driver came to ask if we would consider taking in his recently widowed neighbour. Apparently the man had suffered a stroke six weeks earlier and although paralysed down one side, had just been returned home to an empty flat, after six weeks in hospital. The taxi driver heard him crying for two nights and came to the mission for help.

For a further three weeks we cared for and nursed the neighbour until he died in peace. The dying man said to one of the staff, "I knew I was safe when they wiped the tears from my eyes."

*****

We took in a lady with a brain tumour, who was screaming in pain because of the lack of suitable medication. Another eighteen-stone lady was only with us six days before she died, and an elderly, frail

Nanna, who was on the streets with nowhere to live says, she hopes she will never have to leave the Mission, unless it is in a wooden box!

*****

In contrast, I looked into the face of a man one day who was beaming with joy.

"Would you mind if I took your photograph?" I enquired, as I wanted to record his beauty.

"No problem, you can do as you want as long as you tell the world what God has done for me." *"Go and tell the world what God has done for me,"* he insisted with a smile so big it would have thawed an iceberg.

For two years this man had attended hospital, his body racked with pain, his hands and arms covered in sores. He said he felt like a leper when the doctors told him they could do nothing more to help.

"Tell me how far do you walk to come here each day for prayer care?" We used to wash his hands in a bowl of warm disinfectant water and then pray under our breaths as we gently dried his hands.

"Kilometres," he replied, "but I would willingly walk twenty."

Such was the delight of the humble man sitting in front of me. As I looked into his face I could see the obvious joy. This man had been without hope when he stumbled into the mission building. But when God chose to heal him as encouragement to all of us, He did not take into account our lack of medical experience. He only proved faithful to His own word through faith in the name of Jesus Christ. '*The Spirit of the Lord is upon me. Because the Lord has anointed me; He has sent me to heal the broken hearted; to proclaim liberty to the captives; and the opening of the prison to those who are bound, to proclaim the acceptable year of the Lord.'*

*****

We have since received a nine year old refugee boy from Kosovo into the Hospice unit. This young child, along with his family, was homeless living in a refugee camp. The young boy one day went outside the compound and had a car accident, which sadly put him in a coma with the need to be drip-fed. After a time in hospital the medical profession said they could do no more for him. Their prognosis was; the child would not live much more than a further couple of months, so he was brought to the mission for hospice care for his final days.

*****

At the time of the first edition of this book being published in 1999, we were still praising God that the child had gone from strength to strength. He left the Mission six months later and he was able to say in English, 'thank you Jesus.'

So for all who send financial gifts, please know your sacrifice really makes a difference.

Today the phone calls come in.

"How is the work going on out there?" That seems like a simple enough question, but I wish the answer were as easy.

I believe the whole area of the Balkans is probably one of the greatest mission challenges of our time. With the vacuum left after the breakdown of Communism, and various political and religious groups jostling for power, it is not surprising the whole area of the Balkans has become one of the world's toughest spiritual battlefields.

Bosnia is a bit like an iceberg. There are more dangers lurking under the water than one can first see. This bureaucratic, legalistic pool is the home of some of the world's most damaged people. These people are not only war victims still nursing deep unhealed scars but they are also trapped social victims.

The average man in the street is trying to survive in this furtive breeding ground where control is gained by using one of Satan's greatest tools – fear. Fear coupled with a sense of hopelessness can totally immobilise the strongest of men. Add to that a nation where the largest percentage of families relies on a small social payment. One can then begin to understand why people still walk around using every available means possible to survive.

We missionaries plant the seeds of forgiveness, whilst at the same time we are trying to chip away at the mountain of poverty.

Our calling does not win popularity, because it challenges the strongholds of darkness. It is without doubt, front line spiritual warfare all the way.

Sadly, we often need to pass through the valley of grief before our hearts are pliable enough to become the channels of healing unto the nations.

Can you imagine how heartened I was during one Sunday service? After I had, in simple form, given a gospel message, I asked the children to draw a picture about what they had heard. One little boy, Dennis, drew a cross, with people positioned around the base of it, and a big bag hanging from the cross members.

"What's that big bag hanging on the cross, Dennis?"

"It's a bag of sin," he said triumphantly.

"Well that's a big bag of sin for one small boy," I gently teased.

"Jacqui, don't be silly. It's not all my sin." My eyes filled.

I turned to the second boy and his picture. Again the picture was of a cross but this time there was a wreath of flowers draped over it.

"Please tell me what does your picture mean?"

"Well Jacqui. The flowers are a 'thank you' for what Jesus did for all of us."

Finally the highlight came for Paul, Juso and I when we responded to a request by the Mayor of the town, to visit a man in the final stages of cancer. His grown up Muslim sons were in denial of his impending death, unwilling to be open on the subject. I could see this denial was holding the father in a further place of pain.

After weeks of daily visits, we eventually grasped the opportunity and asked for the privilege of praying with the father. He was delighted.

"Heavenly Father we thank you and praise you for this man's life."

"Amen," he interjected.

"Lord we thank you for giving him the blessing of wonderful children and grandchildren."

"Amen," he responded for the second time.

"And Lord, we want to ask that you will send the comfort of your Holy Spirit to his wife, giving her strength at this time."

"Amen." He was now getting quite excited as the presence of God filled the room.

"And Lord, Heavenly Father, we really want to thank you, that you loved us so much, that you stood by, as your only son was crucified, to take our place as your sacrificial lamb." With that his voice resounded in a mighty, "Amen!"

I don't know how close that came to a sinner's prayer but I do know the peace and happiness which filled that home.

Isn't our Heavenly Father wonderful? Only He could have written such a perfect script confirming His Word through our lives.

I may not know a lot in life, but I do know, I had never read a book until at the age of thirty-five years when a man gave me a copy of the King James Bible.

Today I know that, if Paul and I can make a difference, anyone can step out with whatever amount of faith they possess and trust their Heavenly Father to do the rest.

It is easy to see that this handful of worn out workers need your ongoing prayer support. We want you to know how vital and how thankful we are, for all your prayers and financial help towards the mission's work. You may find yourself one day asking:

"When did we feed you, clothe you, visit you Lord?" And Jesus will answer. "When you did it unto the least of mine...you did it unto me." We are simply your hands and feet.

With love to all our faithful supporters and our Bosnian family, all of whom are so precious in the sight of God. jr

Footnote.

Paul and Jacqui continued in their love towards Jenny until the day she died, and through her twilight years, she and Jacqui continued praying together. Jenny was tireless in her care of others and her life clearly represented the Saviour whom she so loved.

Ricki went on to get a place at Sheffield University England, where he studied mechanical engineering. He eventually went on to graduate and today in 2012 he is married to a Bosnian girl and is a proud father.

Jacqui's father having been absent out of her life for seventeen years finally came home and to faith in his latter years by receiving the love and forgiveness of his Saviour and family. Together they built a strong bond; he died before the work began.

In 2002 the mission building was handed back to the local government for demolition. Government offices now stand on the site.

Today if you ask Jacqui what would be the desire of her heart, she would tell you that she longs to have enough funds to purchase another building for the people. The local town's people have remained faithful and today, twenty year's later Jacqui, despite a lot of physical pain, continues to go out to Bosnia.

It is still the support of Paul and the Faithful few which enables this dynamic love in Christ to continue.

...only God can finish the final story
      because we want Him to receive all the glory.

If you would like Jacqui to come and share their powerful testimony please contact her direct on:

jryalls@toucansurf.com

Donations will be received with much appreciation made out to:

Mission Ministries in Faith.
c/o N.T.C.G. Offices.
40, Nursery Street, Sheffield, Yorkshire, England, S3 8GG.

Tel. 01670 761751.

Registered Charity 1096594.